Discovering
ENGLISH FURNITURE
1720—1830

John Bly

Line drawings by Robin Ollington

Shire Publications, Tring, Herts.

CONTENTS

INTRODUCTION

By the beginning of the eighteenth century, the furniture being made in England can be said to belong to one of three main categories. The first includes the finest pieces, made to the most up-to-date designs by appointed craftsmen for royal and aristocratic households and introducing a new style or a new decorative motif. Second is the furniture made in London and larger towns throughout the country for the moderately wealthy squire and merchant class. This reflected less accurately the introduction of a new style but, because of the sheer quantity made, it laid the foundations for a rapidly expanding furniture industry and forms the bulk of what is today recognised as antique furniture. The third category is the country or cottage furniture made by a retained joiner on a large estate for the houses of the tenants, or by the village carpenter for the cottages of the local people.

By 1720, the craft of furniture making had become a complex industry employing joiners, turners, carvers, gilders, clock and barometer makers, mirror glass makers, fine metal workers and upholsterers. In London and other major cities each branch of the industry became a specialised but integral part in an ever-expanding trade. Construction became the finest in the world, matching even that of furniture made for the French court, and design developed in many ways, with changes influenced by contemporary Europe, by our own historic revivals and by the study of Classical styles. By the 1730s the timber most used for good quality furniture was mahogany and, as had happened with walnut following its introduction, it was used for some time in the solid rather than being cut for veneer. Mahogany lent itself admirably to the skills of a good carver and was a considerable encouragement to the growing taste for the flamboyant Baroque and later Rococo styles, c. 1730 to 1760.

The decade 1720-1730 saw important changes in the design of English furniture and the materials used in its manufacture, but the overlapping of both these aspects occurred to some considerable extent from 1715 to 1745. From the Restoration in 1660 to the later years of Queen Anne, changes in design, methods of decoration and manufacture occurred very quickly. One style ousted another, and affected the countenance of even middle class furniture, quite rapidly. The same cannot be said for the ensuing thirty years. Although mahogany became the standard timber for good quality furniture during the 1730s (see pages 11 and 12) and there was a growing preference for Rococo, the production of walnut furniture did not suddenly cease and furniture of the previous architectural style, particularly wall mirrors and cabinets, following the publication of Palladian as well as Rococo and Gothic designs in 1740.

By the 1720s most household articles that we now take for granted were already in use; some of the more notable exceptions are discussed on page 13. It is therefore the difference in style, construction and decoration which make it possible for us to date and authenticate articles of the first half of the eighteenth century, rather than the article itself or its use, which are so often guiding factors in other periods.

The gentle curves of the Queen Anne period continued with little change save slight modification through the reign of George I, but by the late 1720s fashion had changed and furniture of the first quality was made to one of two styles, and completely opposed styles at that—the Baroque and the Palladian (see page 6). The Baroque was by far the more expensive to produce and therefore much more furniture was made in the Palladian manner. Many of the architectural motifs of the latter could be incorporated in middle class furniture and, for a while, Palladian furniture was the height of fashion. But a seed of favour for the unrestrained had been sown by the elaborate Baroque, and from this grew the hybrid Rococo. From the 1730s the Rococo movement developed, greatly encouraged by the publication of the works of the more fashionable designers, the earliest of whom were practising cabinet makers. This is evident when the designs for furniture by William Kent the architect (see page 7) are compared with those of Matthias Lock the maker and carver. Undoubtedly the most quoted of the mid-eighteenth century designers and craftsmen is Thomas Chippendale (see page 8). His *Gentleman and Cabinet-Maker's Director* included fashionable designs for both ordinary and the most elaborate furniture.

The twenty years from 1740 to 1760 were the great age of mahogany furniture, so much of which can be seen to reflect the Georgians themselves and the times in which they lived. The proportions of the furniture are invariably faultless. Mid eighteenth century tables had wide-spread feet in comparison to the size of the top; chairs had good wide seats; tallboys (chest on chest furniture) had tops narrower than bases and bases narrower than feet, and to retain the balance a large overhanging moulding and cornice was placed on the top.

Even the country made pieces have great charm, probably because the designs of the period lent themselves to more simple manufacture without losing their essential character. Unfortunately this observation becomes less true as the century progressed. Country made furniture of the last quarter of the eighteenth century gained little from the severe lines of classicism.

4

The timber employed was usually the cheaper, softer and more open-grained Honduras mahogany or native woods and, while these were much used for veneers and were suitable for curved patterns, strict alignment and straightness was needed for the successful representation of the designs of Hepplewhite, Adam and Sheraton. Because it was basically easier to produce, a vast amount of unattractive but authentic middle class furniture dating from the last part of the eighteenth century is available today, but it lacks a fineness in its proportions and materials.

By the 1750s a considerable vogue for the Gothic and the second Chinese styles had developed. While both of these can be modified for the decoration of English furniture in a most delightful way, their combination with the Rococo can be over-powering. One of the finest examples of both combined and separate second Chinoiserie period decoration is at Claydon House, Buckinghamshire. Here the Chinese Room contrasts strongly with the combined Palladian, Rococo and Chinoiserie decoration on overdoors and frames of alcoves in the adjoining rooms. The Gothic movement was influenced by Horace Walpole and so typified by his house Strawberry Hill that pure Gothic decoration of this period is often referred to as 'Strawberry Hill Gothic'. Many of the motifs, such as cluster column legs, arched brackets and carved battlements, found their way on to more ordinary furniture, but like Chinoiserie, when combined with Rococo much of the essential charm of Gothic was lost.

It would appear inevitable that following the initial introduc-tion of any one extremely popular design, improvement is piled upon improvement until little of the original remains. This was particularly true of the Rococo movement, which by 1760 had run to wild excess and progress now lay through drastic change. This took the form of an overriding passion for the Classical, modified for suitability in all fields of the decorative arts, princi-pally by the architect and designer Robert Adam.

EARLY GEORGIAN

Design and designers, 1720-1760

William Kent (1685-1748) was the first English architect to revolutionise the plan of our houses and design the furniture to go into them. About 1710, during a period of pronounced taste for Italian architecture, sculpture and paintings, popularised by people returning from the Grand Tour of Europe, William Kent was sent to Italy to study painting. He returned to England in 1719 and thereafter received constant patronage from Richard,

Fig. 1: The five orders of Classical architecture, from left to right: Doric Composite, Tuscan, Ionic, Corinthian. Great importance was attached to a detailed knowledge of Classical architecture in general and these orders in particular by designers and craftsmen during the eighteenth century, and variations are shown in design books of the period. Those illustrated in Chippendale's 'Director' are not fluted, but the basic proportions must remain as the original. Apart from the decoration to base, cap and entablature, each has a specified size. e.g. Corinthian and Composite are ten diameters high, Ionic nine diameters high, Doric eight and Tuscan seven.

third Earl of Burlington. Kent's houses each had a large entrance hall approached from outer steps, and a succession of rooms leading one into another. These great Palladian houses, with their accent on classical lines, porticos and the five orders, Fig. 1, of which Houghton Hall and Holkam Hall in Norfolk are fine examples, had their interiors designed in the same manner. Door pillars and cornices or 'over-doors', although made of wood, had the lines and proportions of masonry as did much of Kent's furniture, which often lacked the feeling of that designed by a man used to working with wood. His book-cases and cabinets, with columns at the sides and architectural cornices and pediments on top, allowed no consideration of the colours and shading of timber. He did, however, advocate considerable use of part or 'parcel' gilding for the tops and collars of columns and the edges and crestings of cornices, and thereby produced an effect peculiar to this period. Kent also made considerable use of ponderous and ornate Baroque designs for many large console tables, mirror frames and chairs, Fig. 2.

6

Fig. 2: An example of a side table in the Baroque taste, c. 1730, in the manner of William Kent. The supporting frame for the marble top would have been decorated with paint, gold or silver leaf, and clearly shows the attempted effect of stone masonry rather than woodwork, a feature strongly apparent in many of Kent's designs.

Fig. 3: A carved console or side table, c. 1745, showing the development from the heavy Baroque to the more gentle Rococo style. It shows a definite French influence and would therefore be more likely to be of pine or lime decorated with paint or metal leaf rather than polished mahogany as on a pure English example.

Baroque and Rococo

The word Baroque, applied to furniture, meant any whimsical, idealistic, asymmetrical design of ponderous proportions. Heavy carved scrolls, eagles with spread wings, masks, torsos, amorini, huge sea shells and other fantastic motifs accentuated with gilding and enriched with fine brocades and velvets were the fashion in France and Italy during the last half of the seventeenth century and early eighteenth century, and gained an important but limited popularity in England particularly after Daniel Marot and William Kent. Magnificence without elegance might be a suitable summary.

The word Rococo is derived from the French *rocaille*, meaning freely 'rockwork', and is used to describe in England what was really a refined simplification of Baroque, with rocks, garlands and festoons of floral motifs used for both the background and the highlights of the decoration, see Fig. 3. The Rococo style originated in France; Pierre Lepautre, whose work c.1700 gained considerable recognition, Claude Audran (1658-1734), Nicholas Pineau (1684-1754) and later J. A. Meissonnier (1696-1750) were among the leading figures of the Rococo movement. The Rococo style continued in England during the early 1740s and remained the predominent fashion for nearly twenty years. The two men who pioneered the English version of this French

7

Fig. 4: A design for a torchere or candle stand showing the uncontrolled decoration suggested for fashionable Rococo furniture from 1745 to 1750. Being more typically English, this stand would have been polished mahogany.

style were Matthias Lock, carver and gilder, and his aide, H. Copland. From 1740 the design books produced by them incorporated asymmetrical and symmetrical carving of all manner of motifs, the C scroll playing a most important part, see Fig. 4 and Plate 6.

One of the most fashionable cabinet makers, certainly of the second quarter of the eighteenth century, was William Hallet (1707-1781). He was employed by Lord Folkestone, the Earl of Leicester, the Earl of Pembroke and, it is believed, by the Duke of Chandos during the building of Canons, near Edgware, described by Defoe as 'the most magnificent palace in England'. In 1745, the Duke's vast fortune having been dissipated, his successor demolished the house and sold the materials and fittings. Hallett bought the estate and much of the materials and built himself an elegant house on the site of the old one. Hallett's son William predeceased him and his grandson, also William, inherited the estate and Canons. By 1786 the grandson had reached such a social position his portrait with his wife was painted by Thomas Gainsborough and entitled *The Morning Walk*. Canons is of greatest interest in this text because it was one of the earliest recorded uses in large quantity of the newly imported timber, mahogany, for the construction of the doors and panelling.

Thomas Chippendale: Rococo, Gothic and Chinoiserie

Thomas Chippendale was born in Yorkshire in 1718, the son of a joiner on a country estate. It can be assumed that he was sent to London as an apprentice cabinet maker for little is known of him before 1748, when he married Catherine Redshaw at St. George's Chapel, Hyde Park. He rented large premises including workshops, a timber store and a front shop in St.

Martin's Lane where he entered into partnership first with James Rannie and secondly with Thomas Haig. In 1754 he published the first edition of a book of designs entitled *The Gentleman and Cabinet-Maker's Director*. This contained 160 fine line engravings showing every conceivable type of furniture decorated or formed after the Rococo, Gothic and Chinese tastes. It included many fantastic creations which were probably never produced, but most important, it showed designs for more ordinary household furniture with some of the fashionable motifs as integral parts of the structure. The open fret cut bracket, the 'cluster column' leg, the carved frieze of icicles, or the arch shape open back of a chair are some typical examples. The *Director* was the first publication to be devoted to furniture alone, and the inclusion of designs which could be achieved by the country craftsmen as well as those for the city carver and cabinet-maker made it a great success; the following year a second edition was published. A third and enlarged edition appeared in 1762, being a compilation of a weekly series issued from 1759. However, some of the finest work to come out of Chippendale's own workshop was not made to designs published in the *Director*. By the early 1760s a Classical revival had begun to replace Rococo and it was for the designer and architect Robert Adam that Chippendale produced furniture of outstanding quality and fineness, reviving the use of marquetry to interpret classical motifs in a display of controlled craftsmanship unsurpassed before or since.

Although the practice of Japanning furniture had continued since its introduction to this country during the latter part of the seventeenth century, the taste for Chinoiserie declined during the early part of the eighteenth century. It revived, however, during the early 1740s, being encouraged to a considerable extent by the wide circulation of books on foreign travel. One of the most influential of these was the magnificent work on China by the Frenchman J. B. du Halde, the English version of which was published during 1742 in weekly instalments. Furniture made in the Chinese manner was for the most part carved and the surface decorated with paint, lacquer, or gilding, or left plain to show the beauty of the wood. The frames of mirrors, torcheres, cabinets, bookcases, tables, chairs and all manner of household fittings were constructed with pagoda-shaped tops, figures of Chinamen, long necked birds (called ho-ho birds), blind and open fret cutting in the style of Chinese fencing, Fig. 5, and often incorporated some Rococo motifs as well. Therefore mid eighteenth century Chinoiserie can be seen to have become more complex in design and freer in concept than the original.

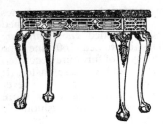

Fig. 5: A mahogany fold-over top card table, c. 1750. This shows the combination of the Rococo and Chinoiserie patterns of decoration. The carving, which stands well proud of the outline of the knees, the cabriole curve, the ball and claw feet, and the carved top edge are made to contrast strongly with the Chinese style blind fret carving on the frieze. Blind fret was produced in two ways during the eighteenth century: the surface is carved in low relief up to a depth of a quarter inch, or is applied with pierced fret cut pieces of wood the same thickness. Through-piercing or open fret was mostly used for chair backs, bookcase pediments and panels in the sides of clock case hoods.

Likewise, eighteenth century Gothic became more eclectic during its most popular period. Gothic taste took as its theme medieval styles, following either a pattern reminiscent of church and cathedral design or of the early castle and its interior. Gothic taste in design had been in evidence since the early 1720s having had only a mild popularity compared to the sweeping Palladianism, but from 1740 to 1765 it reached its eighteenth century height (see Strawberry Hill Gothic, page 5). It would appear to have been a purely English phase, for there are no records of a similar fashion on the Continent, and it is strange that at its greatest popularity, through the romantic designs of Batty Langley, Thomas Chippendale and several other contemporaries, Gothic taste became so fanciful that it bore little if any relationship to its origins. The Gothic style which was revived again during the 1800s showed a much more realistic appreciation of true medieval design, especially in George Smith's *Household Furniture*, published in 1808 (see page 49).

However, mid eighteenth century Gothic is important in this text for like all the preceding designs, it left us with several peculiar motifs which found their way into the furniture of the time. The legs of pot stands, night cupboards (commodes), tables and chairs, etc., might be formed as 'cluster columns', Fig. 6. Open fret-cut corner brackets and chair backs had simulated church window shapes as their basis and the cornices and friezes of cabinets were often embattled.

Walnut and mahogany

Walnut had become the most popular timber for the construction and, later, the decoration of good quality English furniture

Fig. 6: A cluster column leg, one of the most popular design motifs for English furniture made in the Gothic taste c. 1740-1760.

during the last forty years of the seventeenth century. To supplement the insufficient supply of English walnut we had come to rely on European walnut, considered to be of superior quality and imported mainly from France. Unfortunately a very hard winter in 1709 killed much of the continental walnut and in 1720 its export from France was banned. However, by this time we were also importing walnut from Virginia in North America. Virginian walnut is more like mahogany than English and European walnut, having a straighter grain and often attaining a greyish colour which at first glance appears similar to a faded mahogany. It does not however have the depth of colour or the more attractive markings of the other timbers, and was used more in the solid than for veneer. References made to mahogany in the furnishing of Canons, contemporary bills of lading and other manuscripts, and the considerable amount of mahogany furniture extant that dates from 1730-1750 suggest that the changeover from walnut to mahogany was fairly rapid and occurred around 1730 but walnut continued to be used well into the 1750s, but it was no doubt a minority demand.

In 1721, in order to boost the shipbuilding industry, the British Government abolished the heavy import duty on timbers grown in the British colonies in North America and the West Indies. Among these woods was mahogany (genus *Swietenia*) of which the first type imported to this country and used for the construction of furniture came from Jamaica. This 'Jamaica wood', as it was known, had a close grain with attractive markings, a deep reddish colour, and was found to be more durable than walnut. Also the enormous trunks provided wider planks and the timber was less given to warping and shrinking. It was

11

ideally suitable for carving, and when polished (see page 63) showed great depth of colour. Its almost metallic qualities were not confined to strength, for over the years fine examples of early mahogany furniture have attained an appearance closer to bronze than wood (see Patina, page 63). As mahogany became more popular, other sources of supply were discovered, and we began importing it from San Domingo, Puerto Rico and Cuba. As these islands were all Spanish colonies, the wood from them was called Spanish mahogany, although the Cuban timber, which was much used toward the middle of the eighteenth century, is usually catalogued separately, for it provided more varied grain markings while retaining the other important properties of the earlier Spanish woods. Towards the latter part of the eighteenth century we were importing vast quantities of mahogany from Honduras, but this is easily distinguished from the Jamaican, Spanish and Cuban timber. It is much lighter in weight, has a less attractive appearance and less depth of colour, and has an open grain. It filled the tremendous demand for wood for the middle class furniture produced between 1760 and 1820, but was rarely if ever used as show wood on any fine quality work. By the 1740s mahogany had become the fashionable wood and, like walnut, was used first in the solid and then as veneer. The great age of fine mahogany furniture was the middle of the eighteenth century, with the development of elegant designs by men who knew and loved the timber with which they worked.

One important feature to appear on the curved legs of furniture during the early part of the eighteenth century was the 'ball and claw' foot, Fig. 5. This was essentially an Oriental design symbolically portraying the dragon's claw holding the pearl of wisdom. It was used in walnut and then in mahogany furniture until the 1760s, but went out of fashion after the Classical revival. Sometimes the claw of an eagle was used instead of a dragon, and both versions ran concurrently with the pad foot which was already established as a most suitable design for country furniture. The shape of what we term the cabriole leg was actually a double curve which, when reduced in height, made the ogee shape for the bracket feet of chests of drawers, bureau cabinets and bookcases and, during the late 1740s and 1750s, of commodes. By the 1720s it had become the general practice to form the feet of such furniture with a straight sided bracket with some shaping to each end, Fig. 7b, a practice which continued until very nearly the end of the eighteenth century. After the 1730s and usually on better quality furniture, the ogee bracket, Fig. 7a, became more popular and remained so until the 1770s.

12

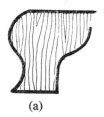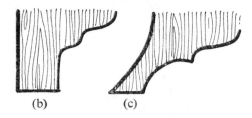

(a)   (b)   (c)

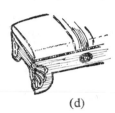

Fig. 7: (a) The ogee bracket foot, popular for
fine quality chest and cabinet furniture from
c. 1740-1775. (b) The plain bracket foot, most used on
more ordinary household furniture from c. 1720-1780.
(c) The splay bracket foot, used for fashionable chest
and cabinet furniture from c. 1780 to 1810. (d) A
Regency bracket foot in the
manner of Thomas Hope,
shown here with the applied
anthemion or formal
honeysuckle motif. c. 1805-
1825. (e) A late Regency
seat end and foot, showing
stylised foliate lowrelief
carving. A similar shaped
foot was also produced with
a turned 'bun' during this
period, c. 1820-1835.

(e)   (d)

Washing stands and night tables

In 1724 Messrs. Gumley and Moore recorded making three
tables of mahogany, one 'supping' and the other two 'desart'.
This is not only one of the earliest references to mahogany in
the manufacture of furniture but it also gives an indication of
the now numerous and diverse uses for which articles of furniture
were being made. During the 1740s and 1750s several items of
furniture first began to appear in quantity. Two such pieces
were washing stands and night tables which by the 1760s had
become standard equipment for the bedrooms of every well-
appointed house. The earliest types of washing stands are
sometimes called wig stands, Fig. 8, and night tables are referred
to as pot-cupboards, Fig. 9, or, the larger type, commodes,
Fig. 10.

The manufacture and use of soap had been known in this

13

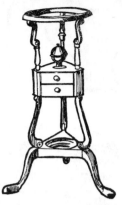

Fig. 8: A tripod base washing stand, often referred to as a wig stand, c. 1750. The top ring held the basin, the lower platform the ewer and above the drawers the spherical cup held the soap which was made in round lumps and known as a wash ball.

country since the fourteenth century, but it was not until the latter half of the seventeenth century that a full cleansing toilet became part of a daily routine, and even then only for a minority

Fig. 9: A mahogany night table or pot-cupboard c. 1800. This type of table was most popular toward the end of the eighteenth century and like the wash stand, Fig. 12, was often made to fit into a corner.

Fig. 10: An English night table commode, c. 1770. The front two legs are divided and the drawer pulls out, supported at the back by the runners, to form a seat. Towards the end of the eighteenth century the top doors were often replaced with a tambour shutter. This is a series of thin strips of wood glued to canvas which can be pushed back into the sides of the cupboard compartment.

14

Fig. 11: A wash stand of the enclosed type c. 1780. Popular from 1760 this type of stand followed to some degree the fashionable decoration of the periods and can often thereby be dated with fair accuracy.

Fig. 12: A corner wash stand, c. 1790. The top is hinged on one side and when raised is supported by a spring clip on the second quadrant which forms a splash-back when open and folds out of sight when closed.

of the population. The introduction during this period of brushes for cleaning teeth and the beginning of an interest in personal cleanliness and appearance suggests that the small occasional table in the bedroom would have had its single drawer full of washing requisites as well as cosmetic preparations (see *Discovering English Furniture 1500-1720*). In addition, from c. 1685 until the early part of the nineteenth century, it was fashionable for gentlemen to shave, and from 1720 it was proper to wear a powdered wig. Thus social behaviour added two more reasons for further development in the furniture industry. Despite the earlier demand there are to date no known authentic examples of stands or tables made specifically to hold jugs and washing bowls prior to the 1740s when two main types were being made. One has a folding top which encloses the bowl and soap compartments, Fig. 11, the other is of triform shape and quite open. It has a circular ring for the bowl supported by three generally curved uprights above one or two triangular shape drawers; these were on three similar supports terminating on a triangular platform which was usually turned or dished to accommodate a pitcher or small bowl, Fig. 12, and the whole thing was raised from the floor by three curved legs. As the soap was produced in round lumps, and was known as a 'wash ball', a small turned spherical cup and cover was often fixed in the centre of the platform above the drawer(s) as the soap box. When this was made detachable, a hole was bored in the base of the cup which then fitted on to a peg fixed to the platform. This type of stand is commonly known today as a wig stand, the theory being that the wig was put on its block, placed in the bowl and then powdered; when not in use the block stood on the bottom platform.

During the second quarter of the eighteenth century the pot-cupboard, night table, and commodious armchair were introduced as a development from the close stool. This type of enclosed chamber pot and seat had been used in large houses and castles since the latter part of the fifteenth century, and during the seventeenth century had become disguised as small trunks and chests. During the first half of the eighteenth century they were usually in the shape of a lift top box with side carrying handles and on four plain bracket feet, either of walnut or later mahogany. Toward the middle of the century close stools were of two main types. One was a small cupboard supported on four tall legs, the other was a larger cupboard with a deep drawer below, of which the front two legs were split and the drawer housing the chamber pot could be pulled out to provide a seat. The commode chair was a large, open frame chair with a loose upholstered seat frame covering the pot which was concealed from the front and sides by a deep shaped rail. One reason that for many years night tables have been referred to in England as commodes was that most of the finest examples of the later eighteenth century were made to look like small chests or cupboards for which the French name was *commode*. This word essentially describes a low chest with drawers, which unlike the English type of chest of drawers is wider in relation to its height, and, being made only for the finer houses, was always the object of the most elaborate or fashionable decoration. After the middle of the century the serpentine and bombe shapes, Fig. 13, were much used for the construction of commodes in the French taste, and two doors often replaced the drawers to form a cupboard. The highest degree of skill and accuracy was needed to make a commode and those that can be seen in museums and country houses today afford us with a close look at the work of many of the leading cabinet makers and designers of the eighteenth century. When describing a fine eighteenth century chest as a commode, stress or accent is on the first syllable—*com*mode; an Engish night table has the stress on the last syllable—com*mode*.

Chest furniture

From the 1740s the basic concept of chest furniture did not change. The tallboy with a chest of two short and three long drawers on a high cabriole leg stand was being replaced by the

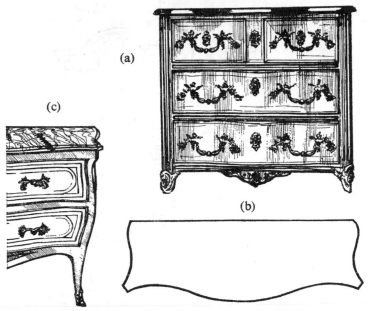

(a)

(c)

(b)

Fig. 13: (a) A mahogany serpentine-shape front chest c. 1755. Strong
French influence is apparent in the construction and proportions of
this chest, and so it might well be described as a 'commode'. Also
shown is the Serpentine shape in plan (b) which when used
three-dimensionally is called 'bombe' (c).

Fig. 14: A double door bureau-cabinet.
The basic shape of this piece of
furniture remained the same through
the transition from walnut to mahogany
and was made as shown from c.
1720-c. 1750. During this time the
doors had either wood panels (blind
doors) or mirror glass. After 1740
separate panes of glass, secured with
astragal mouldings, became popular for
what are generally known as
bureau-bookcases. On the example
shown here the simple backplates to the
handles are typical of the early George
I period; so too are the overhanging
drawer fronts and their arrangement.
The inclusion of a candle slide under
each door is also a mark of good
quality.

17

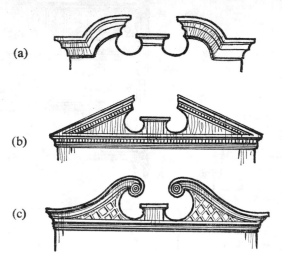

(a)

(b)

(c)

Fig. 15: The development of bookcase and cabinet cornices.
(a) 1700-1730. (b) 1725-1770, the architectural broken pediment.
(c) 1765-1790, the swan-neck cornice shown here with open fret
carving in the recessed panels. This type was popular for the crestings
of fine mirrors as early as c. 1730.

mid 1730s by one with the base part made of another chest of
usually four long drawers on ogee or plain bracket feet and the
top cresting became flat, Plate 7. The bureau-bookcases and
cabinets, Fig. 14, with either blind (solid wood) or glazed doors
to the upper half had similar feet but the top cresting remained
an important feature on those of better quality until the 1790s.
As a general guide—not to be taken as a definite rule—until
c. 1750 these crestings were architectural and most later ones
became deeply curved in what is known as a swan-neck cornice
and often incorporated pierced fret cutting in the recessed panels,
Fig. 15. This type had been used for mirror frame crestings since
c. 1730. The blind doors were panelled and framed either in
straight rectangular form or shaped, the latter being described
as fielded panel, Fig. 16. The glazed doors progressed quite
quickly from plain rectangular frames of six, eight or ten panes
of glass with substantial moulding, to a much finer tracery effect
with delicate 'astragal' mouldings separating the glass, Fig. 17.
From 1760 on, glazed doors for furniture attained an unsurpassed quality of design and construction, and as such could
be made in the Chinoiserie, Gothic and Classical patterns as

18

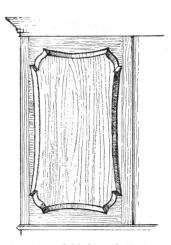

Fig. 16: A fielded panel. Various outlines incorporating this chamfered edge were used to decorate blind doors on cabinets and wardrobes from c. 1730-1770.

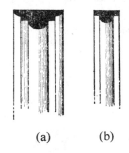

(a)   (b)

Fig. 17: Astragal mouldings. Used correctly the term astragal describes a semi-circular moulding or bead in architecture, but it has for many years been applied to the glazing bars on English cabinet furniture. The types shown are (a) first half of the eighteenth century, becoming finer as in (b) second half of the eighteenth century.

well as the more usual geometric type, Figs. 18 and 19. Of the latter, those having thirteen or fifteen separate panes of glass in each door are regarded as being of better quality. One significant change during the 1730s in the appearance of chest furniture was the shape of the drawer fronts. Following the practice during the early walnut period of placing a single reeded moulding on to the carcase of the chest round the drawer opening, the moulding disappeared, and the drawer front was made to overhang approximately a quarter of an inch all round the drawer. This was formed with a fractional step and a quarter circle section, Fig. 20. In many cases the overhang was on the bottom and side edges only, a simulated moulding being worked on to the top edge, thus giving the appearance of shallower drawers and dispensing with the nuisance of the top lip which could snag or catch when the drawer was used. This method of drawer construction continued well into the 1730s and was therefore used on mahogany and Virginian walnut chests of the period. However, by this time a new construction had been introduced, the application of a 'cock bead'. The earliest known examples of this date from c. 1730; therefore it can be safely assumed that a piece with cock beaded drawer fronts will have

19

Fig. 18: A break-front glazed door bookcase of the type which became popular after c. 1740. By this date such cabinets were made in three parts, the end wings being generally set back to give the break-front effect. The illustration shows a flat moulded cornice, Gothic tracery formed by astragal framework to the glazed doors, and a plain plinth base, c. 1760.

Fig. 19: A mahogany cabinet on chest, c. 1750. The date is confirmed by the rectangular pattern of the substantial glazing bars or astragals and the formal architectural pediment, coupled with the fine quality construction of the chest of drawers base.

Fig. 20: The moulding of the overhanging drawer front which became worked into the top edge of the drawer front prior to c. 1735 when the cock-bead became more popular.

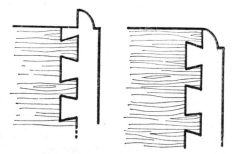

been made after 1735, allowing a few years for the idea to spread and be accepted as an improvement. As can be seen in Plate 29 the drawer front is now flush with the carcase and recedes fully into the opening. It is marked however by a thin semi-circular moulding which protrudes up to one eighth of an inch all round the drawer. This can best be described as the extended edge of a frame of veneer, and its application formed the final phase of the construction of the drawer. It proved to be completely satisfactory, for the cock bead remained the standard finish for drawers of good quality furniture throughout the remainder of the eighteenth century. A poor substitute often found on cheaper articles is a line simply gouged out to simulate a cock bead but this is easily discernable and is the mark of, at best, a country made piece.

Dining tables

By the beginning of the eighteenth century it had become fashionable to have a separate room in which to eat. This had occurred during the Restoration period and was encouraged by the plans for houses in the Palladian style by William Kent. It seems strange therefore that little importance seems to have been attached to the designs of dining tables until the second half of the century. There are to date no known published designs specifically for dining tables before 1750, and authentic examples of this period strongly reflect this apparent lack of interest. They are essentially functional in proportion and appearance being relatively undecorated in comparison with other household furniture of the time, and in design follow a natural progression from the gate-leg table which remained popular until the early 1720s. By the 1730s the gate framework had disappeared on fashionable dining tables, and the folding leaves were supported by legs which swung out from a knuckle joint secured to the underframe of the table. At the top the legs were either round in section or square with a caddy moulding on one corner to the depth of the frame. From there the leg was plain round, tapering to a pad foot. On finer examples the cabriole leg was used and this too terminated in either a pad or ball and claw foot, Fig. 21. With the latter a carved shell, lion mask or other contemporary motif might be introduced on to the knee of the cabriole, but this is rare and the mark of high quality. The most common type found today is the oval top, club or pad foot, drop-leaf table which can date from 1735 to 1760. The next development was to make the leaves of the table rectangular and add an extra free-standing table to each end to accommodate more people. The ends were generally D shaped or semicircular, and when not joined to the centre

Fig. 21: A drop-leaf dining table c. 1740. The form of folding top and swing-out supporting legs had developed from the gate-leg table and was superseded as a dining table by the centre pedestal type during the middle of the eighteenth century. The drop-leaf table of this period is more often found today with a plain cabriole or turned and tapering leg ending in a pad foot.

part could be used as side or pier tables. It can only be surmised that sometime during the 1740s the legs spaced at intervals around the edge of the table annoyed someone so much that he ordered a dining table constructed in the same way as the then popular tripod base china or tea table, but with four spreading legs instead of three, for by 1750 it is known that dining tables with several centre pedestals were produced. As the century progressed, the shape of these centre pedestals and the splay legs followed the fashionable designs of the period, but strangely the drop-leaf centre with additional D ends and turned legs returned to favour during the early years of the nineteenth century. The centre column table continued to be made, for by this time smaller oval and rectangular tables which we now call breakfast tables were becoming popular. This type of table was a small version of the dining table and could be used for less formal occasions in other rooms.

Breakfast and tripod tables

The term breakfast table correctly describes a table suitable for one or two people at which full breakfast could be served. Considerable importance has been attached to this meal since the fifteenth century, and by the middle of the eighteenth century the most popular type of breakfast table had a rectangular top, a leg at each corner and two shallow drop leaves supported when open by two or four lopers which folded out from the underframe. A stretcher platform was built two-thirds of the way down the legs, and the sides and one end of the table were encased by grills of wire or wood fretwork. The open end was fitted with two doors which were often recessed to give knee room and the compartment was used to contain the china or silver ware. A drawer incorporated in the underframe immediately

22

Fig. 22: A breakfast or china table, c. 1750. The leaves of these tables are supported on lopers that swing out from the frame, the legs do not move. The drawer held napery and the compartment encased with wire or fret work, shown here in the Chinese taste, held silver or china utensils.

Fig. 23: A pembroke table with serpentine-shape top, fluted frieze and turned and fluted legs, c. 1775. The supporting lopers which swing out from the frame are shown.

below the top held the napery, Fig. 22. Most small tables without the enclosed compartment but with the drawer and shallow drop leaves are known as pembroke tables and first appeared during the middle of the eighteenth century. They remained popular for the following fifty years and reliably reflected the changes in style and decoration, Fig. 23.

The curved leg terminating in a ball and claw or a pad foot, which for the major part of the first sixty years of the eighteenth century had been the most popular design for both town and provincial furniture, was displaced in favour of straight untapering legs of square section, sometimes with the inside corner chamfered, Fig. 24, for those designs following the Gothic and Chinese tastes. It disappeared completely on fashionable furniture with the Classical revival during the 1760s, to return shortly after in a modified version of a French influence commonly attributed to George Hepplewhite. But while chair and most table legs changed quickly from curved to straight (being easier

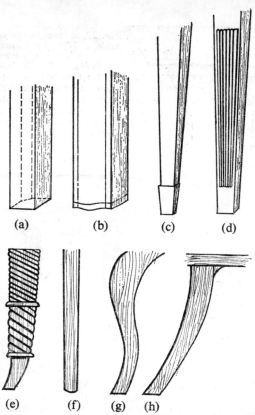

(a)   (b)   (c)   (d)

(e)   (f)   (g) (h)

Fig. 24: The development of chair legs from 1750 to 1820. (a) The straight untapered leg with the inside corner chamfered. Often the ground for blind fret work in the Chinese or Gothic manner, or left plain for country furniture, 1750-1765. (b) The straight moulded front leg 1760-1780 which retained the moulding and became tapered c. 1770-1790. (c) The plain taper leg terminating in spade foot, from c. 1775. By 1800 the spade foot had become less popular and the taper leg was decorated with cross-banding and/or stringing. During the early Regency period reeding (d) became popular and is considered more typical of the period than fluting although both were used. Reeding is convex, fluting is concave. (e) Fine and heavy spiral turning and a circular section splay foot, early 1800s. (f) and (g) The return of the elongated ogee curved leg with semi-circular moulding to the front, and straight sides, first quarter of the nineteenth century. (h) The Grecian curved or sabre leg, first quarter of the eighteenth century.

24

and cheaper to make) one article through its very nature did not abandon the cabriole-type curved leg until much later in the century—the tripod table. The table shown in Plate 2 is typical of the turned centre column, three legged table that must surely have been used in every house in the country throughout the larger part of the eighteenth century. Like all definitely shaped articles of household furniture, it had a fine quality and fashionable prototype. This was the dished or tray top china, tea, or supper table which generally superseded the four legged, oblong type during the late 1730s. The tops were dished (slightly sunken) with a raised edge, or had an applied gallery supported by spindles. The baluster shape turning of the column follows the outline of the baluster supports for the stairways and galleries of Palladian houses and is also the basis for the designs of contemporary coffee pots, hot water jugs and tankards. As the century progressed, it is possible to discern small changes in the basic design of this type of table. The baluster shortened into a ball knob which was later 'cut in half' to form perhaps the most popular of all stems, the spiral turned cup, Plates 2 and 3. The carving on the knees and the inclusion of the open carved Rococo motive make it possible to date this tripod as c. 1745. The 'gun-barrel' stem of the centre kettle stand in Plate 4 had been a standard pattern since the late seventeenth century but was not generally used on more sophisticated mahogany furniture until the second half of the eighteenth century. The combination of this feature with the curved tripod base suggests the stand is therefore country made, not being of the finest quality, c. 1740. The candle stand on the left in the same Plate 4 shows the influence of the Gothic taste in the reverse curve legs and some geometric carving at the base of the pillar. The stand on the right is a Victorian simulation.

A Chippendale period tripod table of finest quality had considerable carving on the base and a dished top with probably a shaped rim similar to the border of a good 1750 period silver salver. In fact, the effect was intended to simulate a tray on a stand which, being pivoted on the block under the top, could be tilted upright to stand against the wall when not in use. The vast majority of tripod tables made in the provinces were of course quite plain and genuine eighteenth century dished top tripod tables are rare. But during the early 1900s, furniture of this period was extremely popular and a great many plain tripod tables entered the workshops of skilled fakers to reappear carved and dished. See Fakes and Alterations, page 67. The 'birdcage' top illustrated in Plate 3 enabled the table to revolve as well as tip up but although it is accepted as a mark of quality a table without a 'birdcage' is not necessarily inferior.

Fig. 25: The sideboard incorporating drawer and cupboard compartments developed from the serving table and pedestals c. 1780. The latter continued to be made for the finer houses, and by the later Regency period, sideboards with built-in pedestal ends (Plate 22) rather than tall legs became popular.

Dining room furniture

Prior to the middle of the eighteenth century the average dining room contained virtually no cupboard space, the napery being brought in by the servants, the cutlery contained in knife cases, and the plate remaining on show on one of the side 'board' tables. In the larger houses these followed the pattern of the other side, pier or console tables in the room and often had a marble top. For the more average household any suitable table was used. By the 1760s however, serving tables with urns on plate warmer cupboards at each end were introduced, and by the 1780s these were incorporated into one piece of furniture, the sideboard, Fig. 25. This development coincided with the introduction of a host of items such as plate carriers, dumb-waiters, wine coolers, cheese coasters, bottle sliders and cellarets.

A dumb-waiter is a two, three or four tier stand on a tripod, Plate 5. The tiers were formed of circular revolving trays graduated in size and supported on a central column. As the name suggests, dumb-waiters were introduced to stand in the dining room to hold additional foods and cutlery for later during the meal when the conversation might become indiscreet and the servants had been dismissed. The best examples follow the contemporary designs of decoration from the 1740s onwards, for although they are mentioned before, dumb-waiters were not generally popular until after that date. Good quality examples have the trays dished, and a thin unwarped tray shows the maker's careful choice of fine timber. From the lower tray up, each column should unscrew, making the replacement of a broken tray a simple operation. The quality and colour of the timber will usually show if this has occurred recently. During the latter part of the eighteenth century and particularly during the Regency period the bases of dumb-waiters often incorporated complicated sections with drawers and compartments and followed the classical and later heavier styles.

There is often some confusion between a dumb-waiter and a what-not, Plate 24, probably because during the later nineteenth century the designs for both were frequently similar. What-not describes a set of usually rectangular trays one above another with the supports at the outer edges and often incorporating one or two drawers in the base. Following its introduction during the last fifteen years of the eighteenth century the what-not was made in various sizes and to all manner of designs.

Still more confusion has arisen regarding the definitions of wine coolers and cellarets. Both these pieces were made to hold bottles of wine and the confusion may well have occurred because during the latter part of the eighteenth century the cellaret was often constructed to serve as both holder and cooler. The earliest known wooden wine coolers or cisterns are c. 1730 and are formed as long open basins lined with lead. They contained ice or very cold water and held the bottles of wine to be served during a meal. After c. 1750 the most popular type was constructed in the same way as a barrel, the sides being straight and sometimes tapering, shaped oval or round and hooped with bands of brass. A tap was inserted at the base and the whole thing was made either to fit into a four-legged stand or to rest on a sideboard pedestal. Cellarets are lidded boxes of oval, round, hexagonal, octagonal or square shape. The interiors are divided into compartments to take a certain number of bottles and, being fitted with a lock and key, they were initially intended to hold a small stock of wine in the dining room at all times. Cellarets came into general use during the 1760s, were lead lined, free standing on feet or legs with castors, and were used extensively until the 1780s when a cellaret drawer was first fitted into one end of the sideboard. The larger and more important types of cellaret continued to be made until the mid-Regency period, but more often with a tap in the base and were therefore used as coolers as well as containers. The ice used was natural frozen water gathered from lakes or pools in winter and stored in deep pits.

Canterburys, Davenports, etc.

Small stands for containing specific items were numerous, often being individually commissioned and later gaining general popularity. One example of this is the Canterbury. According to Thomas Sheraton the Canterbury is either an open box-like stand partitioned to take music, or a shaped stand on tall legs to hold plates and cutlery. The latter is generally referred to today as a plate stand, but the original name for both types is supposed to have derived from the Primate who first ordered the manufacture of such pieces. The Davenport writing desk illustrated in Plate 16 is another example. This type of desk dates from the last part of the eighteenth century and is first recorded as being made by Messrs. Gillow for a Captain Davenport. Davenports became popular during the Regency period and, following contemporary designs, were made throughout the nineteenth century. The later types lost the sliding top which formed the knee space and were constructed more like school desks, with the sides supported on turned or scroll columns.

Another writing table that became extremely popular at the beginning of the nineteenth century was the sofa table. This is a long version of the pembroke table with the two leaves at the narrow sides of the top hinged to form drop ends, Plate 15. The underframe of the top contains two or four shallow drawers and is supported by a pillar at each end with two splay feet terminating in brass cap castors. The original purpose of this type of table was to provide a writing surface which could be drawn over the end of the sofa, Fig. 29; therefore the earlier examples have the strengthening rail high off the ground or arched in a suitable manner. Very soon the rail was lowered and, as it was now visible, decorated to match the rest of the table. During the Regency period, sofa tables with a centre column, shaped platform and curved legs became more fashionable and this type, in gradually increasing degrees of heaviness, remained popular until the 1840s.

By the 1760s most middle class houses had a separate withdrawing room, dining room, hall, reception room and, in some cases, a library. Each of these rooms had to be furnished in the best manner possible and a host of smaller occasional furniture appeared. Breakfast, tea, supper, pembroke and ladies' writing tables were made. For the dining room a dining table, set of chairs, dumb-waiter, wine cooler, cellaret, serving table, plate warmer and probably a large leather draught screen were required. The hall contained at least one console table with pier glass over, hall chairs, a pair of torcheres and a large centre table. And the library had a drum top table, library steps, reading chairs, and a pair of celestial and terrestrial globes. Double chairs, settees, night tables, chests of drawers, bureaux with secretaire rather than slope front compartments, hanging shelves, and wall and corner cupboards went to make up the rest of the appointments in the well-furnished house.

GEORGE III (1760-1820)
THE AGE OF CLASSICISM

Robert Adam

The accession in October 1760 of George III, grandson of George II, had little effect on the sweeping change of fashion from Rococo to Classical. Indeed such was George III's preference for the simpler things in life that he soon gained the nickname of 'farmer' George, and it was left to the fashionable architects, designers and manufacturers of the day to produce and advocate any changes in style and taste. Classical designs had been a steady influence on architecture and, to a certain degree, furniture since the 1720s following the influence of William Kent. However, by the early 1760s the work of Robert Adam, who had been completing his architectural education in Rome with the study of antique designs and decorations, began to have a visible effect on current fashion in this country. The baths of Caracalla and Diocletian, Hadrian's villa at Tivoli, the basilicas and vaulted temples at Herculaneum which Adam visited in 1754, were all to affect the work of English craftsmen within the next ten years. Adam's designs were a definite personalised version of the Classical, whereas Kent's adhered much more strictly to the original. It is interesting to note that at the end of the eighteenth century a neo-classical movement occurred (1799-1830) wherein the designs produced deviated hardly at all from the Roman and Italian models. But the basic idea was the same—simplicity and elegance in outline, and the appearance of height and space and the use of geometrically balanced curves and tapering columns. Adam designed houses and their interiors to incorporate such motifs as husks, urns, festoons, anthemion or honeysuckle, and rams' head masks in the door furniture, wall hangings, mantlepieces, overdoors and cornices, as well as in the carpets, furniture, silver, fine cut glass and porcelain. A particular example of the way in which Adam's designs influenced every field of the creative arts is the contemporary work of the potter Josiah Wedgwood.

George Hepplewhite

For furniture Adam decreed various forms of surface decoration which enhanced and accentuated rather than detracted from the essentially simple and elegant outline. Much of the early Classical period furniture shows the use of incised and applied carving on plain mahogany, but by 1770 veneer work had again become popular and so too had its natural partner marquetry. Some of the finest marquetry of this period was executed to designs of Robert Adam by Thomas Chippendale and John Haig, Plate 12. But furniture made strictly to Adam's designs was intended only to go into the great country and London houses where he or his contemporary followers were employed at the time. And just as the Rococo, Gothic and Chinoiserie styles had been presented to furniture makers throughout the country by Thomas Chippendale, so the designs of Adam were spread to a far wider field by the work of George Hepplewhite. Comparatively little is known of this man, and it is largely because of the three hundred illustrations published in his *Cabinet Maker and Upholsterers' Guide* in 1788, two years after his death, that his name is so well known. That he had practical knowledge of a workshop is substantiated by the fact that he was at one time an apprentice to the firm of Gillow of Lancaster and by 1760 had established a shop in Cripplegate in London. The *Guide* was actually published by Hepplewhite's widow Alice, and was such a success that a second edition was published in 1789 and a third in 1794. Hepplewhite only incorporated those designs of Adam he thought most suitable for furniture. There appear no military trophies or rams' head masks on Hepplewhite's designs. Excluded too was the use of classical scenes painted in panels forming the focal point on an article. He made use of oval and round paterae (carved and usually applied discs), swags, husks, flower and bell festoons, and fluting, and although he did not invent he certainly popularised the heart and the shield as shapes for chair backs. He almost certainly introduced the use of simulated Prince of Wales feathers as a motif, although the idea might have stemmed from the designs for some chair backs by James Wyatt, a young and successful architect of the period. Running concurrently with this was a strong

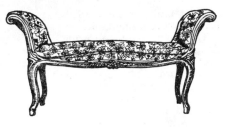

Fig. 26: A window seat c. 1780, showing French influence in the curving frame. Small window seats were more popular in England after 1775.

French influence which can be seen in the curving lines of small window seats, Fig. 26, and open armchairs of this style between 1770 and 1790. As this was, like most influences, a modified version attributed to a leading designer of the time in this country, it is generally referred to as 'French Hepplewhite'.

Thomas Sheraton

Straight tapering legs, delicacy of framework and general fine proportion in furniture continued and improved until the end of the eighteenth century, reaching its zenith during the 1790s. The designs of Thomas Sheraton in his *Cabinet-Maker and Upholsterer's Drawing Book* (published in three parts from 1791 to 1794) are the best examples of this. Sheraton was born in Stockton-on-Tees in 1751 and is believed to have come to London during the early 1790s. He was trained as a practising cabinet maker but there is to date no proof that he actually made furniture to his own designs. He was an extremely competent draughtsman and author of various works on philosophy and religion. But his *Drawing Book* presents us with the most comprehensive picture available of good quality furniture of the late eighteenth century. It was regarded in the same way by contemporary craftsmen all over England, and for the most part his designs were faithfully reproduced. Thus the majority of good quality furniture of this period is today recognised as being 'Sheraton'.

Sheraton took for his designs points of style and decoration from his predecessors and contemporaries and, blending them in a most delightful way, produced designs of unique elegance in English furniture. After the turn of the century, Sheraton became more affected by the formal Classical movement and in 1803 published the *Cabinet Dictionary*. In this he illustrated the French and Grecian styles, and advocated much use of animal figures, torsos, heads and feet as important features. This affected both fine and more ordinary furniture, a typical example being the plain brass cap type of castor, Fig. 31, which became realistically cast to represent a lion's paw. This pattern remained

31

popular until the early 1820s, at which time an acanthus leaf became more fashionable.

The tremendous following that fashionable architects and designers had during this period means that there must have been an unprecedented number of extremely wealthy patrons. This in turn can be related to the economic situation in England which had gone from strength to strength under the Whig administration. The signing of the Treaty of Paris in 1763 had signalled the end of the Seven Years War with France and had opened up new areas for commercial expansion, hence more French influence. The pattern of higher social behaviour also contributed to the vast amount of domestic articles produced to a set design during this period. Great interest in history and the arts in general promoted circles of friends to follow particular lines of study, so various groups covering large areas of the country attained considerable uniformity within themselves.

This can be easily understood when considering the complex social pattern which developed during the last quarter of the eighteenth century, with so many different influences vying for popularity and each gaining sufficient importance to affect in some degree even the more ordinary household article in some particular piece of decoration.

It is possible to imagine by the end of the eighteenth century in England a complex society similar to that of today. There were 'avante-garde' extremists, the more staid aristocracy relatively unconcerned with all but established good taste, the wealthy untitled trying desperately to keep up with both, the middle class managing nicely and the poor, as always, poor and unaffected by fashion. It is therefore difficult to catagorise in chronological order the different tastes and fashions that were at some time popular and important to our furniture history from 1799 to 1825, and the brief description which follows is intended to show rather how much was going on during this period than the chronological introduction of any one style.

Henry Holland

By the end of the eighteenth century a movement for pure Classical designs as against the modified versions of Adam had set in, and what is known today as the Neo-classical Movement began. This was partly affected by and partly coincided with the acceptance of some of the designs of furniture made for the avante-garde Prince George. His importance in the world of design and fashion at this date explains why typical furniture of the period from 1800 to 1830 is generally referred to as Regency, although the constitutional Regency was only from 1811 to 1820. Prince George's architect and principal furniture

1. A mahogany fold-over top card table, c. 1735. The frieze contains one long drawer which has the original combined escutcheon and back plate for the drop handle. The cabriole legs terminate in lion's paw feet, and the carved lion mask decoration at the knee can be seen clearly to stand well proud of the outline of the curve.

2. A tripod base, rectangular top mahogany tea table, c. 1750. Examples of this period often have plain rectangular as well as circular tops: here can be seen the runners and block which enable the top to tip up but not revolve as in the case of a 'birdcage' fitting. The carved square section of Rococo motif on the stem is particularly unusual. The writhen turned cup is above three decorated legs terminating in well formed ball and claw feet. Here too the carving can be seen to stand proud of the outline of the curve.

3. A mahogany tripod table, c. 1750. The pierced peg at the top of the column fits into a bird-cage which allows the table top to revolve and tilt, being secured with a wedge through the slot. The finely turned baluster shape column has the lower part in a writhen turned cup which can be seen to stand proud of the outline of the curve. So too can the carved shell motifs on the knees.

4. Tripod base kettle or urn stands. (Left) Mahogany, country made c. 1755, and interesting for the ringed tapering column, the inverted curved legs and the inclusion of small Gothic motifs at the base of the column. (Centre) Mahogany, country made c. 1755. The undecorated tapering or 'gun-barrel' column is out of period and more typical of country made pieces. Both these stands are too tall to have been made from pole screen bases, often a present day hazard, and the proportions of the small tops on wide spread bases compare favourably with right which is a Victorian version of a Gothic style stand; the inclusion of too many decorative features and poor proportions are the initial guides to the date of this piece. Also it is made of rosewood which makes it unlikely to have been made c. 1760 as its appearance might at first suggest.

5. A mahogany dumb-waiter of two tiers on tripod base c. 1755. From the middle of the eighteenth century dumb-waiters developed in line with other tripod base occasional furniture, having three, four and even five tiers. Towards the end of the century these were sometimes made to drop down like the leaves of a pembroke table being supported by a revolving bar. The tripod here shows a fine example of a plain curved leg terminating in a pad or club foot.

6. A carved wood and gilt mirror, c. 1755. The frame clearly shows the 'C' scrolls combined with simulated rockwork and freely placed flowers. All are fine examples of typical Rococo decoration.

9. (Right) A mahogany dining chair, c. 1760. The pierced back splat shows an increased formality in its almost Gothic design, yet retains three small Rococo features and includes three blind fret lozenges. The fact that the straight untapered legs and the simple arms are left undecorated suggests a country made chair. However it is not uncommon to find one extremely fine portion in an otherwise plain article of this period.

7. A mahogany tallboy, c. 1770. The upper half is surmounted with a wide overhanging moulded 'dental' cornice and has canted (chamfered and fluted) corners. The base has a pull out brushing slide over three drawers and bold ogee bracket feet. The handles and escutcheons are original. Note the retaining moulding is on the base as it should be.

8. A mahogany dining chair, c. 1750. The pierced back splat, shaped top rail and arm supports have carved foliate decoration in the Rococo manner, and the cabriole front legs terminating in bold ball and claw feet continue this theme in the decoration on the knees. All carving can be seen to stand proud of the outline of its curve. The close nailed upholstery finishes above a gadroon edge (spirally lobed), a motif also popular for fine contemporary silverware.

10. (Above) A mahogany dining chair, c. 1775. This chair clearly showing the development from Plates 8 and 9 in the influence of the Classical movement. The serpentine-shape top and lower rails of the back, the graceful pierced splat and the square tapering legs are the important features. The drop-in seat had become popular by 1760.

11. A mahogany open arm chair, c. 1780. The frame and supports for the shield back are moulded serpentine in section; wheat ears and husks are carved on the four splats; the arms and tapered legs are reeded and joined by a short, leaf capped column above carved patera and terminate in well-formed spade feet.

12. *Veneer and inlay decoration of the second marquetry period, to designs by Robert Adam and executed by Messrs. Chippendale and Haig 1772-1779. Veneers of rosewood, satinwood, kingwood, sycamore and harewood (sycamore dyed green with oxide of iron) were used on this secretaire chest. The ends are quartered rosewood enhanced with satinwood crossbanding and boxwood stringing; the secretaire drawer is crossbanded with satinwood, kingwood and rosewood around the panel of formal foliate marquetry which is further enhanced with surface etching, a method of decoration not used on English marquetry until this period. The doors bear quartered rosewood inserted with oval panels surrounded by entwined bands called 'guilloche' borders and classical vases in fields of satinwood. The columns are decorated with honeysuckle motifs and the feet have a panel of*

satinwood over a single Greek key. A secretaire or secretary has a drawer which is hinged at the bottom and when pulled out falls to the horizontal to form a writing surface supported by two brass quadrants, and reveals a set of small drawers and compartments similar to those in a bureau. Secretaires were particularly popular from c. 1770 to 1810.

13. A satinwood bonheur du jour or lady's writing table, c. 1790. In the manner of Thomas Sheraton's earlier designs, this table shows the effective use of quartered and crossbanded veneers and the absence of any marquetry. The finely tapered legs are panelled with a single line of boxwood stringing and it can be seen that they taper from the inside edges only to avoid a 'pin-toed' appearance. Half of the table top is hinged at the front edge and folds over to be supported by the drawer which when open reveals a pen and ink compartment at the side.

14. A rosewood cheveret or lady's writing table with portable book carrier, c. 1795. Like the bonheur du jour, this type of small table was extremely popular during the last fifteen years of the eighteenth century and the Sheraton period. This one shows the use of well figured, but not quartered, rosewood veneer panelled and bordered with fine stringing and satinwood cross-banding. The lower platform with a recessed front edge was a popular feature of the cheveret, and the ivory knobs and spade toe castors are original.

15. A mahogany sofa table, c. 1800. This is a typical example of the plainer but fashionable furniture being produced at this time. The triple reed edge to the top had become popular by the end of the century, and the standard ends well show the plain sweeping splay legs terminating in horizontal cup castors. Contemporary cheval mirrors (tall swivel dressing mirrors) had similar supports and legs, and during the late nineteenth and early twentieth centuries were often 'married' to later Regency sofa table tops which were old but not so valuable as the type illustrated here.

16. *A mahogany Davenport writing desk, c. 1805, decorated with ebonised stringing. The name Davenport is alleged to derive from a Captain Davenport who first commissioned such a piece to be made at the end of the eighteenth century. The one illustrated has an unusual fold-over top, four-reed edges and curved feet in the Regency classic style. The cup castors are original.*

17. *A Regency period mahogany 'breakfast' table, c. 1805. Toward the end of the eighteenth century, tables to seat four, six or eight people for meals in less formal rooms than the dining room had become popular. The oval or rectangular tops were invariably supported on a centre column and splay legs. The late eighteenth century legs swept off the column as shown on the sofa table, Plate 15, but after the turn of the century the curved leg with a knee became popular, growing more exaggerated as the Regency period progressed. The top has a single band of black stringing, the legs are carved in the manner of George Smith and terminate in original lion's paw castors.*

18. *A Regency period mahogany library table with drum top, c. 1810. Such tables became popular during the last half of the eighteenth century, but the ebonised inlay to drawers and legs, the ring-turned column, the pronounced swell to the knees of the legs and the lion's paw castors date the table as early nineteenth century.*

19. *A mid-Regency period card table of mahogany decorated with ebonised inlay of classical motifs, c. 1815. The centre column and platform with the legs spreading from each corner was a popular form for side and centre tables of this period. The top swivelled on the frame and opened across it. This table shows early use of the carved acanthus leaf on the knee and castors.*

20. *A carved wood and gilt mirror in the Regency marine style, c. 1810.
The use of marine subjects for furniture decoration became fashionable
following successful campaigns at sea during the early 1800s, but declined
after 1815. The style was revived to a minor extent after 1835 but the
proportions of the later examples are generally more ponderous.*

21. *A 'carving' and 'single' dining chair of a type most popular in the
Midlands during the early part of the nineteenth century. Production of
such chairs was plentiful at this time, and they were usually made in sets
of up to twenty-four. Distinguishing features dating them before 1825
are the inside top back rail, the veneered panel with brass inlayed stringing, the spiral turned centre bar from which they get the name 'rope-
back', the degree of fineness in the turned front legs, and the moulded
sides and arms.*

22. *An early nineteenth century turned leg sideboard, decorated with well-figured mahogany veneer, c. 1810. The pattern of the legs often matched that of contemporary dining chairs, and like them this form of sideboard remained popular in the provinces until 1825-1830.*

23. *A Regency period pedestal-end sideboard and cellaret c. 1815. The finely figured mahogany veneer is cross-banded and lined out with box-wood and gilt brass stringing. The semicircular turned columns are an unusual feature and a mark of extra quality. The lion mask and ring handles are original, so too are the short curved front legs. It is usual to find turned back feet and curved front ones; by the end of the Regency period both front and back were turned. Occasionally the front feet are so exaggerated that the weight is taken by a block in the centre of the pedestal base.*

24. *A mahogany what-not, c. 1805 Designs for sets of square or rectangular shelves with a drawer or cupboard compartment at the base were divers from 1800 onward. The more typical example has each shelf separated by turned columns similar to those of the lower part in the illustration. This is unusual in the lyre shape supports at the top. The drawer retains a cock bead edge which is repeated on the end panels. The turned wood knobs are original, so too are the carved wood lion's paw feet at the front and the turned feet at the back.*

25. *A carved wood and gilt convex mirror, c. 1805. This type of mirror was introduced from France to England toward the end of the eighteenth century and by 1800 had become extremely popular. Good quality examples are invariably crested by an eagle with a ball and chain pendant from its beak. They were much advocated by Thomas Sheraton in his 'Cabinet Dictionary' of 1803 for the attractive light reflections created by the convex mirror plate. The illustration shows the inclusion of dolphins and bullrushes with a sea-horse at the base.*

26. A late Regency period cupboard with mirror glass back and shelf over, c. 1820. Referred to as a chiffonier, these were often made in pairs, and this one bears many features of the later Regency: the turned and reeded bun feet, the heavily lobed and beaded borders, the moulded side columns capped with formal acanthus leaf scroll, and the stylised lotus leaf at the base of each gilt metal support. The pierced brass gallery and the brass grill to the doors are original. Many later chiffoniers were made with solid wood panelled doors which, to increase their market value, have been removed and replaced with reproduction grills.

27. A late Regency period cabinet in the Classical style, c. 1822. The cabinet is veneered with kingwood and ebonised stringing, and has a cornice more typical of the style of Thomas Hope; however, the freestanding columns to the base and the overall proportions are too heavy for the early Regency archaeological taste and to support this a design for a similar article was published in 1822 by Richard Brown.

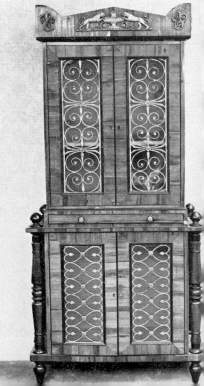

28. *A rosewood dining chair, c. 1828. This chair includes many features of the later Regency which were to set the scene for the William IV and early Victorian furniture designs: the double curved and overhanging back top rail, the formal tendril scroll under, the centre back splat pierced and carved with foliate motifs and the finely carved inverted lotus leaf cap to each front leg. The semi-circular baton front rail is unusual, but one or two unexpected features continued to appear on finer quality furniture until large scale mass-production took over.*

29. *The corner and drawer end of a mahogany chest of drawers, c. 1765. Here can be seen the development of the dovetail joints from those of the early eighteenth century, see 'Discovering English Furniture 1500-1720' plate 2. Note the end of the drawer front is rebated to receive the cock bead which runs all round the edge. When the drawer is closed (see lower drawer) the front is flush with the carcase leaving the cock bead proud up to one-eighth of an inch. This method of decorating drawer fronts continued into the early 1800s, but by the end of the eighteenth century, a single band of boxwood stringing became more popular.*

31. A bird-cage platform shown with the top tilted. This top has an unusual framework of four runners instead of two. A lighter area and four bruises corresponding to the protruding column ends are clearly visible on the underside of the top caused by close contact with the platform when the top is closed. Darker shading is where frequent dusting has created a dull shine. Such a combination of features is never successfully attained by the faker. Also visible are the heads of the fixing screws of the runners and the metal latch and plate.

30. The corner and drawer end of a chest of drawers c. 1805. This shows a good quality piece the drawer linings of which are now mahogany rather than oak. The dovetails are cut much finer, and a line of ebony stringing has replaced the cock bead. The lion mask and ring handles are original, and the four-reed edge to the top support this date.

32. A mahogany work table, c. 1795. The top has a narrow line of satinwood crossbanding and the drawer fronts are edged with stringing. The pendant handles as shown in Fig. 30 are original and the legs can be seen to taper on the inside only.

33.
The inside of the work box shown above and described on page 68.

designer from 1783 until 1806 was Henry Holland, whose designs in the Graeco-Roman and Chinese manners were to affect our furniture history for long after his death in 1806.

In 1783, the year of his coming of age, George, Prince of Wales, received Carlton House as his London residence, and Henry Holland was appointed to rebuild and redecorate it. Thus his Graeco-Roman designs were already established well before the end of the century. These were very much influenced by the French taste of the Louis XVI, the Empire and the Directoire periods, for the French Revolution, the Napoleonic Wars and the Bourbon Restoration were important contributing factors in the complex changes of Regency fashion.

Thomas Hope

To enable the flourishing of the decorative arts there have to be patrons. Occasionally a patron does more than supply funds, and himself makes an important contribution to the arts; indulging a life's interest and a fortune in producing ideas for others to follow as well as the patronage to make it possible. Such a man was Thomas Hope, 1770-1831. While his name is often connected with a minor and somewhat eccentric furtherance of the Egyptian taste, the truth is that Hope produced designs for furniture and interior decoration in the purest Egyptian, Grecian and Roman styles. Essentially these were for his house in Duchess Street, London, and later The Deepdene, near Dorking in Surrey. Both were altered to house his collections of classical bronzes, vases and other antiquities, and the furniture and settings were intended to enhance them. However, in order to encourage this taste, Hope published a book of his own drawings —*Household Furniture and Interior Decoration*—in 1807 (see chart on page 71). This showed his outstanding ability as a draughtsman and designer, from complete room schemes to separate pieces of furniture and individual motifs. He incorporated and popularised many motifs of the French Empire period and the use of black and coloured paint with gilding in the manner of the ancient Egyptians. In fact it is only in recent years that Hope's great contribution to design has really been appreciated.

George Smith

While the original in any fashion remains exclusive, certain modifications will generally ensure a wider appeal. The early nineteenth century was the beginning of an age when more people than ever before were in a position to afford the fashionable material comforts of their choice, and the selection available was the most varied ever known. One of the chief exponents of the modified versions of the classic of this period was the cabinet-maker and upholsterer George Smith. His first major work *A Collection of Designs for Household Furniture and Interior Decoration*, published in 1808, set out his ideas and showed a somewhat light-hearted treatment of classical styles. His excessive use of animal figures, the sphinx, griffins, lions and leopards, and the bold use of anthemion (stylized honeysuckle), acanthus and palm leaf motifs can be said to typify the main essence of the Regency. The revival of lacquer, both Chinese and Japanese, of caning for back and seat panels of chairs, and of buhl, and the continuance of part gilding gave the period tremendous variety.

The Chinoiserie taste of the period was considerably more delicate in form than the two previous periods during the late seventeenth and mid eighteenth centuries. Both Chinese and Japanese lacquer work were popular decoration, especially for door panels of cabinets and cupboards. The essential difference between the two is difficult to describe but easy to see. Basically the Chinese work had a free and almost romantic use of human figures often brightly coloured, whereas the Japanese was more formal, with scenes of sparse landscapes depicted in gold, silver and copper colours and relying to a great extent on simplicity for much of its appeal.

Gothic, Trafalgar and Buhl

During the later years of the constitutional Regency there was a marked decline in the demand for the simple, elegant furniture of the early Sheraton type. Design generally became more bulky and decoration more ornate and heavy. By 1820 there was a strong feeling for the Old French and a Gothic revival, which was to last in various forms for the next seventy years, was well established. While nearly all the books of design for household furniture produced since Chippendale's *Director* had shown one or two articles in the Gothic style, it was not until the later Regency that Gothic became again prominent. This coincided with the decline in the use of marine subjects as decoration or for complete pieces in about 1815, see Plate 20. The inclusion of such features as dolphins, cables, cannon, anchors and shells began at the time of our great naval victories under the command of Lord Nelson, about 1803. His death in 1805 also affected furniture design; the back splats of chairs were carved to simulate the drapery around the admiral's sarcophagus, and it is from this date that a preference for ebony or blackened stringing (see Veneer, pages 59 and 65) replaced the previously popular light and contrasting variety. Dolphins had been important decorative features on fine furniture of the

Fig. 27: A mahogany cylinder fall writing desk with bookcase over, c. 1805. The quadrant section lid folded back into the desk and a writing platform could be pulled forward by means of the second row of knobs. Variations of this type of desk were made after the 1790s. The illustration shows one of fine quality timber, decorated with ebonised stringing, finely turned legs and shallow cup castors.

William Kent period, but the early nineteenth century versions were generally of lighter proportions. Ebony stringing, usually on a ground of finely figured mahogany, remained popular until c. 1815 when lines of brass became more fashionable. At about this time a fashion for buhl decoration began and this too, like the Gothic, remained in varying degrees popular for the next seventy years. Buhl work is a type of marquetry using sheet brass and tortoiseshell and was yet another revival from the late seventeenth century and an influence from France. See page 60. The best known Englishman to work both with buhl and brass inlay was George Bullock, a stonemason, upholsterer and cabinet-maker. For distinctive decorative designs Bullock favoured the representation of both naturalistic and stylized English flowers and was keen to use native timbers. Thus pollarded oak and elm became popular for some fashionable furniture during the mid Regency period.

Old French

From 1820, when the Prince Regent became George IV, until 1830, when he died, taste seems to have gravitated towards

Fig. 28: Two late Regency crestings, showing the use of formal foliage portrayed in a free classic manner 1825-1835.

the Old French, particularly that of the Louis XIV period. With the fashion for buhl, large ormolu or gilt metal mounts often surrounding embossed metal plaques depicting classical scenes became popular (ormolu, page 56). These were mostly incorporated on ebonised furniture such as the long, low cabinets and commodes that continued to be made for the next sixty years, although the later almost mass-produced models are of a vastly inferior quality. Also during this time the woods of mahogany and oak became used more in the solid, and in general less furniture was painted although gilding, to emphasise some decorative motif, continued.

The use of classical motifs on the more ponderous furniture of the late Regency gave way to the use of carved, stylized floral motifs on much the same basic shapes. The lotus leaf, which was a popular motif of the period, is a particularly notable example, see Fig. 7e on page 13. Designs for furniture and interior decoration of this period are probably best typified and illustrated in George Smith's last publication of 1828, *The*

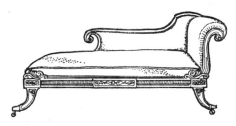

Fig. 29: A Regency period sofa, c. 1810. The terms sofa, couch, day-bed, chaise longue, settle and settee all describe long seat furniture. The first four are generally used today to describe such pieces on which the sitter may recline, whereas settles and settees are seats for more than one person. The word sofa first appeared in this context in England at the beginning of the eighteenth century and chaise longue appeared during the 1790s. The illustration shows the half back single end sofa over which a sofa table might be drawn.

Cabinet Maker's and Upholsterer's Guide. Herein are designs for sofas and sideboards, bed drapes and curtains.

By 1830 the taste for the Old French was under way. In 1827, Crockford's Club had its interior decor redesigned in the Louis XIV style by Phillip and Benjamin Dean Wyatt, and within three years the French taste had become popular for most fashionable bedrooms and boudoirs; while the heavier and more formal 'Modern Greek' was still considered proper for the masculine apartments. It is with these two overriding styles that the complex pattern of the Victorian age began, to change rapidly with the introduction of more and more ancient English and foreign influences in a period of industrial invention and the greatest exhibitions the world had ever seen.

Decoration and materials

During the latter part of the eighteenth century English furniture made in mahogany and in the French taste was usually left undecorated. Any decoration used was either of gilded gesso, i.e. the application of gold leaf on to a previously prepared surface of whiting and size, (see *Discovering English Furniture 1500-1720*, page 25), or painting with white or pastel colours which could be enhanced with gilt. Pine and lime were found to be more suitable to receive gesso and paint than mahogany, and both woods were much cheaper. This guide does not apply to furniture made in the Classical taste of the same period. Exotic timbers for veneer were further 'improved' with painted panels depicting mythological and classical scenes by such artists as Antonio Zucchi, Angelica Kauffman, and Michele Angelo Pergolesi. Also at this time, fine marquetry of such timbers became widely used, and the cupboard by Messrs. Chippendale and Haig, Plate 12, is a magnificent example of classical marquetry decoration of this period. The two woods most popularly connected with the last quarter of the eighteenth century are satinwood and rosewood, but there were many others. The species of satinwood used on the finest quality furniture at this time came from the West Indies. It had a fine golden yellow colour, a hard straight grain, and such depth that it closely resembled satin material with an occasional irregularity. This type came mostly from Puerto Rico and was used for veneering on to mahogany or pine until the end of the century when Sheraton suggested its use in the solid.

A second type of satinwood was imported from the East Indies but this did not come into general use for furniture until the early part of the nineteenth century. It had a more shallow, lemon colour with closer, smaller markings, and it has not as yet matured to the richness of the West Indian variety. This type

53

was used extensively in the solid during the late nineteenth century.

Rosewood came from first the West Indies and later the East Indies and Brazil. Like satinwood it was used for veneer and decoration before being used in the solid. It is generally a dark wood with red-brown streaks accentuated by darker brown or black markings. The covering of protective polish (see page 63) that was applied to most furniture at this time has allowed some rosewood articles to attain a mellow and well figured appearance. If this original polish is removed, however, rosewood tends to turn black and much of its beauty can be lost. Three other types of wood having streaky and contrasting grain are kingwood, tulipwood and zebra wood. They were all used as veneers for panels and bandings rather than in the solid. Kingwood is more like satinwood in general colour appearance, but has greater contrast between the dark and lighter deep golden markings. Tulipwood is sometimes confused with rosewood because its tendency to fade lessens the contrast between the dark and light markings which, when the wood is freshly cut, vary from deep red to yellow. Zebra wood is a hard, close-grained timber with fairly close and very pronounced markings of light yellow and dark brown.

Towards the end of the century, to add contrast in figure as well as colour on a piece of veneered furniture, use was made of curly grained wood and burr cut timbers. In addition to those already known such as the burrs of oak, alder, elm, yew and maple, two new types were used; amboyna wood and thuya wood. Amboyna, with its pleasing light brown colour and 'bird's eye' figuring was used extensively for both complete surfaces and banding and was imported from the West Indies. Thuya was imported from Africa and had similar figuring but a much deeper colour than amboyna. During this period, and even more so during the early years of the nineteenth century, an enormous variety of highly decorative timbers were used. They are generally classified as belonging to one of three main recognisable types; those of essentially uniform colour but with great depth, of which certain cuts of mahogany, satinwood, oak, maple, harewood and ebony are the best examples; those with contrasting streaks in the grain such as rosewood, kingwood, zebra wood, tulipwood and coromandel; and those with the burr of pollarded figuring such as amboyna, alder, oak, elm, maple and thuya.

Metal mounts

By the 1750s a separate yet integral industry connected with the furniture trade had developed; the manufacture of metal

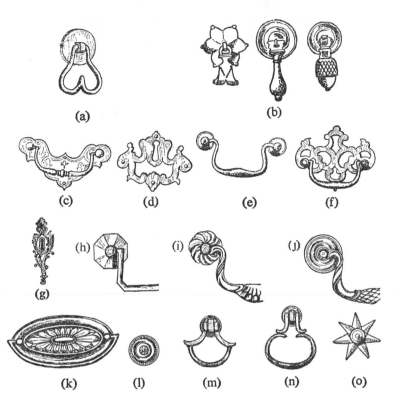

Fig. 30: Some typical handles of the seventeenth, eighteenth and nineteenth centuries.
(a) Iron inverted heart shape drop handle, early seventeenth century.
(b) Brass pendant handles, early eighteenth century. (c) Engraved back-plate loop handle of cast brass, early eighteenth century.
(d) Pierced escutcheon, later part first half of eighteenth century.
(e) Loop or swan-neck handle of cast brass, second half of eighteenth century. (f) Pierced back-plate loop handle, c.1760. (g) Cast brass escutcheon in the Rococo manner, mid eighteenth century. (h) Cast brass loop handle with octagonal rose, French style, second half of the eighteenth century. (i) and (j) Two types of decoratively cast and chased loop handles with roses, later eighteenth century. (k) Stamped sheet brass back-plate loop handle, after c. 1780. (l) Stamped brass knob with screw fixing, late eighteenth century. (m) Cast brass drop handle, c. 1775-1800. (n) Cast brass drop handle, c. 1750-1775. (o) Regency period star knob.

mounts. Iron locks had been used on chests since the fourteenth century. These were the outside plate type, which during the fifteenth century became more decorated. Such advances were made in their manufacture that by the sixteenth and early seventeenth centuries cupboards for downstair rooms had concealed locks with the keyhole protected by a plate escutcheon. Either as part of this plate or fixed separately was a wrought inverted heart shaped handle, which on country oak and fruit-wood furniture was used until the early part of the eighteenth century. During the latter part of the seventeenth century, however, the forging of furniture mounts and locksmithing became separate occupations from that of the general black-smith. The Oriental lacquered furniture that was imported to this country in such vast quantities after the Restoration bore large double plate escutcheons, corner guards and angle straps; naturally, as increasing amounts of imitation lacquered furniture were produced in England the metal mounts had also to be reproduced. For a considerable time the fine quality of the chased decoration on the original eluded the English manufac-turers, but the importance of metalwork on furniture had been established and materials other than iron began to be used, and from the latter part of the seventeenth century brass con-tinued to be the most popular. The development of drawer handles and escutcheon plates is shown in Fig. 30. Until the latter part of the eighteenth century metal mounts of this type were cast from a mould, 'finished' by the chaser and engraver and then either polished and lacquered or gilded. Although gilt metal mounts of the finest quality were produced in France from the end of the seventeenth century, it was not until the 1760s and after that the equivalent or anywhere near it was produced in England. These were known as ormolu mounts and the word ormolu has since become used to describe any gilt metal mounts on English furniture. By the time the word was used in England during the latter part of the eighteenth century, it was discontinued in France in favour of the term *bronze d'ore*. This accounts for the supposition in England that ormolu applies only to work executed in gilt bronze. This is not neces-sarily true; ormolu can be any fine gilt metal, for the derivation is from *or moulu*—ground gold; therefore either gilt brass or bronze can be described as ormolu. The main method of applying the gold was mercurial gilding. This is done by mixing gold and mercury to form an amalgam, applying it to the surface of the metal which is then heated to evaporate the mercury and leave the gold firmly fixed. (This method is no longer used as the fumes from evaporating mercury can be lethal.) The development of the metal mount industry in England, and at one time the sale of English ormolu in France, can be attributed to one man—Matthew Boulton (1728-1802). Boulton was the primary figure in the production of fine metalware and from his workshops in Soho, Birmingham, came clocks, silver plated wares, and ormolu. His mounts were incorporated in designs for the finest furniture by the Adam brothers and their contemporaries. During this time the mounting of semi-precious stone to form such delightful articles as cassolets (decorative candlesticks of classical shape, the sconces of which can be reversed to form pot-pourri vases) became popular. Apart from the changes in design of handles and escutcheons during the late eighteenth century and Regency periods the most significant metal mounts on furniture were the castors or small wheels which enabled a piece to be moved easily from one place to another. A simple form of castor was no doubt in use for some special pieces of furniture as early as the sixteenth century, but the full use of such a fitting was apparently not recognised until the end of the seventeenth century. At this time was introduced a wooden wheel on an axle secured to a pin which allowed movement in any direction, and during the early 1700s small hardwood rollers were used on domestic furniture. By the 1740s and 1750s the rollers were made of leather, being several washers placed together on the axle, and the pin was secured with a brass plate which was screwed to the underside of the foot, Fig. 31. While ball-and-claw and pad feet provided space enough for this plate the tapering legs and feet of the post-1760 period did not. Therefore a cup-type castor which fitted over the end of the leg was introduced. This, which after c. 1770 was all made of brass, was at first straight and later tapered in shape, and those of the 1775-1800 period often represented the spade feet which were so popular at this time, Fig. 31. The cup castor on the horizontal, as in the case of a tripod base, was introduced as an alternative by Thomas Sheraton, and from 1790 to 1830 can give us a good idea of whether or not the fitting is original. The first of this form to appear was basically rectangular with the edges slightly chamfered and followed the end of the line of the leg. An alternative was the same shape with a raised lip. Soon after the turn of the century, a realistically cast lion's paw was the most popular type of castor, but by 1820 this too had gone out of fashion to be replaced by the formal leaf and other typical design motifs of the period, see Fig. 31.

Veneer and marquetry

Veneer is a thin slice of wood applied to the basic structure of a piece of furniture as a form of decoration. It was first used in England during the Restoration period, c. 1670, and was origin-

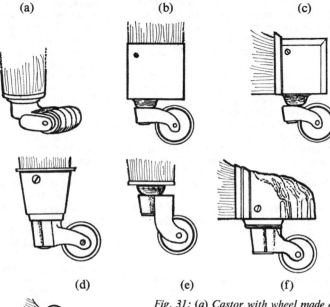

(a)   (b)   (c)

(d)   (e)   (f)

(g)

Fig. 31: (a) Castor with wheel made of leather discs, c. 1740-1760. Used for ball and claw feet and square untapered legs. (b) Square cup castor, c. 1760-1775, by which time it was generally made of brass. (c) The plain toe castor on the horizontal used for the spreading legs of the tripod and four splay table bases. From 1790 if tapered. (d) The tapered cup castor which with a top protruding lip often replaced the spade foot for turned and square legs, from 1785. (e) A small brass castor used on small pieces of furniture during the last quarter of the eighteenth century. (f) The lion's paw castor, 1800-1820, but a most popular replacement for later or reproduction furniture. (g) A typical late Regency stylised foliate cap castor, c. 1820-1835.

ally called faneer, because it was first produced by cutting across the grain, thus showing the 'fan' of the timber, (see *Discovering English Furniture 1500-1750*). The next development was the introduction from Holland of marquetry. This describes a decorative panel or border made up of several contrasting coloured veneers in intricate designs and applied to the carcase as a whole. There are two distinct types of marquetry of this period, see chart on page 70, and both these as well as parquetry and veneer in general continued as one of the most fashionable types of furniture decoration until the end of the seventeenth century. By the early 1700s marquetry and parquetry were less popular and by the 1730s most fashionable cabinet makers were using solid mahogany in preference to walnut veneer. During the Classical period of the later eighteenth century, the import of a variety of exotic timbers encouraged a revival of veneer and, to a lesser extent, marquetry. However, eighteenth century veneer of mahogany, satinwood, rosewood, etc., was generally cut along the grain, that is down the tree, rather than across, and contemporary marquetry also had a feature in its manufacture which distinguishes it from the earlier type. On seventeenth century marquetry the additional details of veins on leaves, feathers on birds etc., which appear to have been scribed on to the wood are, in fact, fine saw cuts, and are made more easily perceptible by the glue having risen through these cuts when the marquetry was applied. Eighteenth century classical period marquetry had such additional detail scribed or drawn on to the wood after the panel had been applied, giving an even finer, etched appearance. This was not done on English marquetry before the middle of the eighteenth century. The designs too were different: the eighteenth century version employing classical motifs, military trophies, shells and quarter fans rather than the scrolling vine, tendril and floral patterns which were popular in the seventeenth century. Quartering the veneer also became popular again, being made even more distinctive with the use of such woods as satinwood, mahogany and kingwood cut along the grain. A fine example of this can be seen in Plate 13. To complete and frame the carefully selected and applied veneers, stringing and crossbanding were also reintroduced. These were found to be ideal for both fine and more ordinary furniture, as the insertion of a line of contrasting colour wood to a plain surface, such as boxwood to mahogany, and an edge of crossbanding immediately gave a fashionable appearance to a mediocre article. Herringbone stringing in its earlier form was not popular: instead, variations of chequer stringing were sometimes used. Both these and panels of wood marquetry went out of fashion towards the end of the century and remained so until after 1850 when their revival continued until c. 1910. During the Regency period, burr veneers were extremely popular, and after 1815 panels of buhl work were used on the finest furniture. The word buhl describes panels of brass and tortoiseshell inlay produced in the same way as marquetry: thin sheets of each material are glued together and the required design, generally of intricate scrolls and foliage, is cut through both diagonally; the glue is melted and the designs and materials can then be interchanged. The two alternatives of background or decoration material thus provided are known as buhl and counter-buhl, and furniture to be decorated in this way was often made in pairs to take both. Folding tea and card tables, wall cabinets, chiffoniers and bookcases are typical examples. Red, deep yellow and green tortoiseshell could be obtained by varying the colour of the surface to which the buhl panel was applied. This method of decoration was first used in England during the late seventeenth century, and derives its name from the originator in France, Andre Charles Boule, see chart on page 70. It did not receive the popularity in England it gained on the Continent at this time, and was little used in England after the first quarter of the eighteenth century. In 1815, however, another Frenchman, Louis Gaigneur, opened premises in London, and supplied to the Prince Regent a writing table decorated with buhl. From then on it remained fashionable in varying degrees, terminating in a deluge of mass production in the 1870s.

FAKES, ALTERATIONS AND IMPROVEMENTS

The title of this chapter summarises the main types of spurious articles likely to be encountered today. An increase in demand for any merchandise inevitably leads to the production of inferior facsimiles, and old English furniture is certainly no exception. This is not a new development. The work of cabinet makers, carvers and polishers of the early 1900s is a memorial to the inexpert but enthusiastic collectors and the unethical or ignorant vendors of that period. Today, therefore, we not only have to be aware of the skilled faker and reproducer of the present time but of the work of such men since the turn of the century. To complicate matters even more there are the items brought up to date in appearance or altered in shape and use by enthusiastic amateurs during the late Victorian period. In an age of tremendous industrial development little respect was shown for ordinary household articles of a past era, and to refashion such items was therefore a justifiable improvement.

However, the motives were at least honest if completely mis-guided. In contrast, during the early 1900s the services of the skilled faker were in demand to appease the appetites of wealthy collectors. Having obtained the finest known examples available, these men sought the unknown and the impossible. Furniture made to designs undreamt of by Kent, Chippendale and Hepple-white was forced into famous collections by pitting the pride of one collector against another. Inevitably several law suits followed during the 1920s bringing disrepute to all concerned.

The complete fake is an article made with old materials, in the old method of construction by a highly skilled craftsman, and produced for the sole purpose of deception. The majority of such fakes were made during the early 1900s, and after fifty years genuine wear and tear their discovery can sometimes be difficult. But while the skilled fakers had a knowledge of the design and styles of the early periods, they were naturally proud of their work and few resisted the temptation of incor-porating a small feature or "trademark" somewhere on the article. This might be a minor addition or omission which would not have occurred on the genuine piece. These fakes were fine articles which, had they been genuine, would have been treated with respect throughout their lifetime and would not show signs of constant use. But once exposed as false, reverence ceased, and half a century of daily handling has added enough appearance of age to confuse even further the furnishing collector of today, for a most important guide to the recognition of a fake is the evidence of use. For many years now the production of this type of fake has been low, the cost of skilled labour and the scarcity of the correct materials making it financially unworth-while. Unfortunately the same cannot be said for the next category, the basically old but improved piece. This describes an article which, while remaining structurally unaltered, has the addition of decoration which would have been applied to only its finest contemporary counterpart. In general terms it describes a plain article converted by decoration into what appears to be a fine article. This was done mostly on eighteenth century mahogany furniture, but there are instances of this type of improvement occurring on country-made walnut furniture of the early eighteenth century.

The next hazard to confront the present day collector is the reproduction. The commercial mass-produced reproduction is made as near as possible to antique design, being slightly modi-fied for use in the modern home, and made with the most up-to-date machinery. This type has been made since the turn of the century, but its very design and proportion are enough to give it away at first or, at most, second glance. The commercial reproduction was never intended to deceive, but to fulfil a demand for antique style at low prices. However, vast quantities of extremely fine quality reproduction furniture have been and are being produced. These pieces are exact replicas of an original, with the minimum use of machinery in the production. Considerable time and skill is employed in research for authenticity of design and the achievement of a suitable patina, but the use of new timber and the absence of any signs of age underneath the article are sufficient for immediate recognition.

The article which has been altered structurally exists, like the recarved or improved piece, for one of two reasons. Furniture was altered during the nineteenth century because its original function was inadequate or size inconvenient, or to falsely increase the value as the demand for antiques increased. Thus bureau-cabinets and bookcases were separated, sideboards reduced in width or length, clothes presses were made into wardrobes by removing the shelves.

Having established the types of fakes most likely to be encountered the next step is to realise the various ways they can be identified. Unfortunately most of the unhelpful remarks inferring that years of study and practical experience are the only ways to learn are for the most part true. However, there are several guides rather than rules which may help to establish whether or not an article needs further examination. The most important single aspect in learning about old furniture is the ability to recognise that something is wrong. Knowing exactly what or where will come with time and experience, and when faced with such a problem piece there should be no hesitation in seeking further authoritative advice. It is equally important to avoid being too hasty in condemning outright an article where some doubt exists. The reason may be no more than an honestly but poorly executed repair. Providing this is not excessive and does not alter the character or use of the article, it may be acceptable.

When viewing furniture formulate and memorise knowledge into brackets or headings which can be brought to mind quickly and easily. For example:

Date plus Shape plus Use plus Material.
Colour and surface condition (patina). Signs of wear.
Construction. Wood behaviour. Unexposed wood condition.

The first four should be compatible and contemporary and will signify the earliest date an article could have been made, i.e. Rococo style after 1730, tripod tea tables after 1720, mahogany after 1725. Having established that date, shape, use and material are contemporary, look for colour and surface condition.

Patina

Since craftsmen first took pride in their work, the outer surfaces of furniture have had some sort of preservative treatment when new. Following the decline in popularity during the sixteenth century of painting furniture after the application of a grain filler, the use of either an oil polish or a polish of beeswax and turpentine became standard practice. The main difference in the effect of these polishes is that through oxidisation the oil polish darkened the wood, whereas the beeswax sealed it and retained the mellow colour. The use of oil or wax polish continued on country furniture until the nineteenth century, but during the early Restoration period the use of varnish became most popular on all fine furniture. The first type of varnish used on most fine and particularly veneered furniture since the latter part of the sixteenth century was an oil and resin varnish. Thin coats of this mixture were applied to the surface of the wood, allowing time between each for the resin to dry out the oil. The surface was then rubbed with any one of a variety of mild abrasives which eventually filled the grain and left the timber well preserved, of good colour and ready for the first beeswaxing. Oil varnish was superseded during the 1670s by a spirit varnish. This consisted of spirits of wine and gum lac and was known as China varnish, introduced to England from the East where it had been used to preserve the fine lacquer work being imported into England at that time. As with the lacquer work itself, the materials were not available in western Europe to make China varnish, but before long we had discovered a suitable alternative. This was basically the same formula with a spirit base but either seed-lac or shell-lac was used instead of gum lac. The method of application was essentially the same as for the oil varnish. During the early 1820s an easier and inferior method of obtaining an immediate lustrous surface superseded the arduous task of varnishing. This was a formula introduced from France called 'french polishing' and consisted of soaking with shellac and spirit a wad or 'fad' of fine linen over padding Several applications of this are made to the surface of the furniture until a glass-like finish is achieved. French polish is not as durable as oil varnish; it chips and wears away and is easily marked by heat or damp.

Unfortunately many pieces of earlier furniture have had the original patina stripped away to be french polished during the nineteenth and twentieth centuries. This detracts considerably from the merit of an article and can often be recognised by close examination of the grain.

To prepare a recently stripped and therefore open grained surface for french polishing the grain has first to be filled.

During the nineteenth and early twentieth centuries ground pea-flower, whiting or plaster of Paris were most often used. These were stained a suitable colour and when dry the french polish was applied. Over the years the stain has bleached, leaving the grain marked with pale brown or white flecks. This does not occur on the surface of English furniture made before the early nineteenth century which retains its original finish or patina.

Whatever the colour of an article, it should have good patination. This describes the condition of the surface after years of waxing, the accumulation of grease and dirt and the multitude of small scratches resulting from general but not careless use.

During the eighteenth century both waxing and varnishing were used for polishing English furniture. Waxing was considered most suitable for chairs and smaller articles constructed in solid undecorated mahogany, and varnishing most suitable for most veneered surfaces.

Over a long period of time dirt and wax have not only filled the grain but have built up into small ridges above the surface. These can be seen when viewed obliquely against the light and cannot be reproduced, thus providing a guarantee of at least an old top, leg, rail or stretcher. On veneered surfaces, the varnish filled and sealed the grain, so there is no raised grain effect. Occasionally, fine ridges caused by the glue pushing through between the lines of stringing and crossbanding can be perceived with the fingertips, but by no means so noticeably as on the walnut veneered furniture of the late seventeenth century, see *Discovering English Furniture 1500-1720*. So for the most part it is the colour, absence of pale grain filler and the other elements of patina mentioned above which are the guides to the authenticity of surface condition on furniture of the late eighteenth century.

Signs of wear

Whereas the signs of use in the patina concern the outer surfaces, signs of wear relate to the effects of handling and the movement of working parts. In order to examine a piece of furniture it has to be lifted up or tilted. When doing this note where the hands automatically take hold and where the ends of the fingers touch. It will have been moved in the same way since it was made and the hands and fingers will reach the same area. Such places should be darker than the rest of the underside. The natural oils of hands and fingers and the gradual accumulation of dust and dirt will have given the appearance almost of a patina. The rest of the underside should be dry looking, paler and perhaps dusty but not stained or polished. This applies without exception to chair and stool rails, drawer linings and table frames. Close scrutiny of the movement of working parts where two wood surfaces rub one against another should always reveal corresponding friction marks. The underneath of drop leaf table tops where the leg pulls out in an arc to support the leaf, drawers and their runners and hinged doors that have fractionally dropped and rub on the frame or rail are typical instances.

While the faker seems to have ignored the simulation of hand holds underneath furniture, he has certainly spared no effort and imagination in achieving an instant patina on the outer surfaces or show wood. The effects of discoloration of most timbers can be gained by using chemicals. For the country faker in the past the most popular and efficient method of achieving age and in particular the rotted away feet and watermark appearance was to stand the furniture in a regularly used stable. The acidity therein speeded the work of two hundred years into a matter of a few months. All manner of implements such as chains and small pieces of clinker as well as the conventional tools of the workshop were used to obtain the bruises and scratches that occur with constant use and form an integral part of the patina. But here too, the enthusiastic faker so often gives himself away by overdoing the 'distressing'. This occurs when signs of use appear on places where it would not be expected and closer inspection reveals the distressing to be regular in pattern.

Veneers

During the late seventeenth and early eighteenth centuries oak was seldom used as background material for walnut veneer, but during the middle of the eighteenth century it was much used in this way for mahogany veneer on better quality furniture. By the end of the eighteenth century mahogany itself was employed as background for veneers of satin wood, rosewood, kingwood, etc., and cedar was often used for the linings of small drawers in the finest quality pieces. The changes in the use of timbers form a pattern. Soft native timbers like deal were cheaper than oak yet adequate to be covered with walnut veneer and so were used in preference to oak. Mahogany, like walnut, was first used in the solid, but by the middle of the eighteenth century demand for fashionable furniture was so great that it was also used as veneer—on oak, for oak was used as background for the best French veneers, and our native soft woods had a tendency to warp. Solid oak had not been used for fashionable furniture for more than seventy years and, being less in demand, was now cheaper. By the end of the century mahogany was plentiful, less expensive, and could be cut to an even greater degree of fineness than oak, and was therefore considered suitable as both background and surface timber for the delicate furniture of that period.

The thickness of the veneer can also be a guide as to whether or not an article has been improved at a later date. Eighteenth century veneer was hand cut by saw, and was rarely less than one sixteenth of an inch thick. During the nineteenth century machine-cutting of veneer developed, and by 1900 paper thin veneers were being produced. An open or unfinished edge, a chipped corner, crack, or a piece of stringing which has come away are some of the places where the thickness of the veneer can be seen.

Just as the recarver improved originally plain eighteenth century furniture when the styles of Chippendale and Hepplewhite were so popular during the early 1900s, so the inlay worker applied his craft to similar pieces during the period of what is now known as Edwardian Sheraton. Whereas the absence of raised carved decoration is a guide to authenticity through the alteration of surface depth, see opposite, the re-inlayed piece provides a less obvious give-away. The wood removed to take decoration is replaced with panels of marquetry, stringing and crossbanding and its surface covered with layers of french polish. But where this has occurred the surface is slightly dented, and can be seen when viewed obliquely against the light. Oval shells, corner fans, box wood stringing and satinwood cross-banding are among the features most commonly employed by the re-inlayer, and it is basically through this man's lack of sense of proportion and ignorance of the eighteenth century original that it is possible to recognise his work. Inevitably it was the cheaper variety of article that underwent improvement and, as such, will always appear odd. Equally, it will have a highly polished surface, and the slightest sign of pale grain filler should lead to much closer examination of the inlay work. Inlay of the eighteenth century was applied to the better quality furniture and produced in the finest possible way. Only the contrasting grains of the different timbers reveal the joints between background and inlay, as if nothing but the thinnest razor blade had been used to cut the timber. There will be no space between the veneers except on previously uncared-for pieces when a minute ridge caused by glue coming through from the back might be just visible.

Alterations

One of the most popular articles to be improved by recarving has been the plain top, tripod base tea table, see page 25. The basic construction for both fine and plain tables of this type was the same. A square or rectangular platform, called a block, with two corners extended to form one inch long circular pegs was fixed to the top of the column. The pegs fitted into holes in the runners which were then screwed to the underside of the top across the grain of the timber to prevent warping. The top was fastened in the horizontal position by a metal latch and plate. Thus the table could be tilted to stand against the wall when not in use. A variation is the bird-cage feature which enables the top to revolve as well as tip up, and which may be found on both fine and plain examples.

In order to establish whether the base and top are contemporary the top should be tilted and the areas where the block, underside of top and insides of runners have been in close contact should be carefully examined. As such tables were more often closed than tilted, these areas will have been less exposed to air and dust and should therefore appear slightly cleaner. Friction marks on the insides of the runners and edges of the block caused when the table has been tilted should correspond. If the metal latch and ends of the tenons or bird-cage columns protrude slightly above the surface of the block, there should be corresponding bruises on the top made when it is closed. Such protrusions will have occurred because the block has shrunk slightly across the grain of the timber, see Plate 31. The fact that timber shrinks across and not along the grain can be a useful guide on many occasions. For example, a tray top is 'dished' on a lathe and when new is perfectly circular; an original eighteenth century tray top rarely is, for the timber will have shrunk slightly; if a tray top is found to be exactly circular it is likely to have been altered recently, and further examination is advisable. An authentic tray top was turned from a thick piece of timber. A top intended to be plain was of thinner timber as there was no need to allow for dishing. Therefore when an originally plain top has been altered to a tray at a later date, the ends of the fixing screws for the runners will have been exposed. These can be easily cut off, but the holes will still be evident. To camouflage these the top will no doubt have been falsely scratched and bruised but their regularity should make them apparent. Note the position of the runners under the top and then carefully examine the top surface for two corresponding rows of eight equally spaced marks. The gallery edge supported on small turned pillars found on fine torcheres and tripod tables from the 1755-1775 period was invariably made in sections to give extra strength, whereas a 'pie-crust' or other raised and shaped edge was carved from the solid, which leads to another important guide regarding the authenticity of decoration. When an eighteenth century craftsman planned to have an article decorated with carving he allowed sufficient timber for the motif to stand proud of the basic outline of the curved leg or rail, see Plates 1, 2 and 3. The recarver or faker had no such opportunity, and had therefore to cut into the already shaped surface to give the impression of relief. If the carving does not appear raised above the outline of a curved surface it is unlikely to be contemporary.

An example of a piece of furniture altered for utility reasons rather than an attempt to increase its value is the small work table illustrated in Plate 33. Originally this had three shallow drawers below the fixed top to hold silks and cottons for needle-work. A subsequent owner has had the upper two drawers removed, the top hinged, a new lock fitted using the existing keyhole in the top drawer, and the drawer fronts fixed to the carcase forming dummy drawers. Old lining paper is pasted roughly over the inside and marks caused when the securing blocks on the underside of the top were carelessly removed are clearly visible. As the hinges are apparently not the first it can be assumed that the alteration occurred some time ago. Similarly, for utility purposes, many articles of household furniture have been reduced in length, width and height; sideboards have had drawers removed to provide cupboard space, spinets have been converted to dressing tables, and many two-piece articles such as bureau-bookcases, cabinets and tallboys have been parted to make separate items of furniture. However, the poor proportions that inevitably result from such alterations are generally sufficient to create a doubt of authenticity. More recently a demand for taller case and cabinet furniture has caused originally single bureaux and secretaire chests to have upper cabinets added. Again proportion is an important aspect, but certain features in the original construction can be useful. The upper part should fit into a retaining moulding which was secured to the base, rarely to the upper part itself, and the top surface of a bureau or secretaire chest that was to be covered by a cabinet was rarely veneered.

Woodworm

The evidence of woodworm is not necessarily a sign of age in furniture. The woodworm belongs to the same species as the death watch beetle and generally attacks furniture in poorly ventilated conditions. Woodworms eat into timber leaving small round holes visible on the surface. They then change direction and rest just below the surface where they go through various phases of development before emerging. Eggs are laid in the spring and the greatest activity is during the summer months. Use of a well-known worm killer is the best treatment, but for severe damage an expert should be consulted. Woodworms burrow in and out of timber, never along the surface, so when any part of a piece of furniture has the surface disfigured with semi-circular channels and worm holes it must have been cut from timber previously used on another piece of furniture. No cabinet maker would have used ugly timber originally, but in an attempt to give 'age' to a piece the faker might.

During the nineteenth century it was fashionable to remove original metal handles and replace them with turned wood knobs. Modern castings of old handles have made it possible to restore the correct appearance to a piece of furniture previously mutilated in this way, and the right style of handle can be gleaned from illustrations in eighteenth century design books. A wrong handle immediately makes a piece of furniture look unbalanced and of bad proportions, therefore a new handle of original shape and style can be considered preferable to a Victorian or later one of the wrong size and pattern.

The points discussed in this chapter are some of the faults likely to be encountered today on furniture of the 1720-1830 period. No one guide should be used alone but in conjunction with the text of the previous chapters and as many other aspects as possible. The inclusion or omission of one feature does not mean that an article is definitely genuine or fake: for instance, the lack of patina with the raised grain effect may have been caused by an enthusiastic polisher in the nineteenth century with no intent to deceive; alternatively its presence means only that the timber has always been the outer surface of something. A sense of proportion plays a large part in recognising that something is wrong, for however elaborate the decoration, furniture of the eighteenth century is always well balanced. It cannot be stressed too strongly that knowledge of the original is of paramount importance. Domestic English furniture was intended for use as well as decoration. Therefore it is only to be expected that working parts such as drawer runners, locks, hinges and woodjoints have become worn or damaged. Honest repair or replacement of such damage is quite acceptable providing it is well done, for furniture should, as far as possible, fulfil its original purpose. Treated with normal care and respect, old furniture can add warm atmosphere and character to a home, and most important of all, it will continue to improve in appearance while providing the owner with a pleasing and tangible piece of English history.

Monarch	Date	Style	Materials
HENRY VIII	1509·1547	**TUDOR PERIOD** Gothic Ecclesiastical Renaissance Designs	**OAK** FRUIT WOODS · BEECH · ASH · ELM FOR COUNTRY FURNITURE
EDWARD VI	1547·1553		
MARY I	1553·1558		LOW RELIEF CARVING · SOME PAINT (TEMPERA) & GUILDING
ELIZABETH	1558·1603	**ELIZABETHAN PERIOD** Renaissance	INLAY USING FRUIT WOODS BEECH · ASH · HOLLY · SYCAMORE BONE · IVORY · MOTHER OF PEARL
JAMES I	1603·1625	**STUART PERIOD** Jacobean Renaissance Classicism	
CHARLES I	1625·1649	Dutch Influence·	TAPESTRY MANUFACTUREY AT MORTLAKE ESTBD 1620
COMMONWEALTH	1649·1660	Puritan Style	**WALNUT**
RESTORATION	1660	**CAROLEAN PERIOD** Restoration Period 1st Chinoiserie	CANE FOR SEATS & BACKS OF CHAIRS · VENEER PARQUETRY OYSTERWOOD · LABURNUM · BOX HOLLY · FLORAL MARQUETRY
CHARLES II	1649·1685	Spanish Influence Netherlands	USING HOLLY · FRUIT WOODS BURR WALNUT · EBONY ETC
JAMES II	1685·1689	Huguenot Influence	CARVED LIME & PINE FOR GESSO & GILDING · SILVERING ORIENTAL ENGLISH LACQUER
WILLIAM III MARY	1689·1702	Dutch Influence	ARABESQUE "SEAWEED" MARQUETRY USING BOX OR HOLLY & WALNUT
ANNE	1702·1714	Baroque	SOLID WALNUT
GEORGE I	1714·1727	**GEORGIAN PERIOD** Palladian Revival Baroque	**MAHOGANY** JAMAICAN · CUBAN
GEORGE II	1727·1760	Roccoco Gothic 2nd Chinoiserie	
GEORGE III	1760·1820	**CLASSICAL REVIVAL** French Taste **REGENCY PERIOD**	HONDURAS PAINTED FURNITURE SATINWOOD · KINGWOOD ETC EXOTIC WOODS FOR VENEERS MARQUETRY REVIVAL
REGENCY	1811·1820	Græco Roman Neo-Classical	
GEORGE IV	1820·1830	Empire · Trafalgar 3rd Chinoiserie Egyptian	GILDING · LACQUER & BUHL
WILLIAM IV	1830·1837	Old French · Gothic Early English Revival	
VICTORIA	1837·1901	**VICTORIAN PERIOD** Gothic (Mediæval) · Rustic Modern English · Art Nouveau Japanese	VARIOUS MATERIALS · PAPIER MACHE
EDWARD VII	1901·1910	**EDWARDIAN PERIOD** Queen Anne, Sheraton Chippendale Style Reproductions	

Time chart of styles and materials

Principal Designers	**Principal Makers**
INIGO JONES 1573·1651 THE ENGLISH PALLADIO' ONE TIME SURVEYOR GENERAL OF ROYAL BUILDINGS TO JAMES I & CHARLES I	**GERREIT JENSEN Circa 1680·1715** CABINET MAKER TO THE ROYAL HOUSEHOLDS OF CHARLES II & QUEEN ANNE
FRANCIS CLEYN DESIGNER AT MORTLAKE 1623·1658	**JOHN GUMLEY 1694·1729**
DANIEL MAROT Circa 1662·1752	**JAMES MOORE 1708·1726**
Wm KENT 1686·1748 (Palladian)	
	ANDRÉ CHARLES BOULE 1642·1732
Thos CHIPPENDALE 1718·1779 1ST EDITION OF HIS GENTLEMANS & CABINET MAKERS DIRECTOR PUBLISHED 1754 2ND 1755 3RD 1763	**Thos CHIPPENDALE 1718·1779**
Robt ADAM 1728·1792 CLASSICAL INFLUENCE FOLLOWING HIS RETURN TO ENGLAND IN **1758**	**Thos CHIPPENDALE Jnr 1749·1822** IN PARTNERSHIP WITH THOMAS HAIG 1771·1796
BATTY & THOS LANGLEY PUBLISHED IN 1740· CITY & COUNTRY BUILDER'S & WORKMAN'S TREASURY OF DESIGNS · FRENCH STYLE & GOTHIC	**MATHIAS LOCK 1740·1769** VARIOUS PUBLICATIONS CIRCA 1740·1769 CARVER AS WELL
Geo HEPPLE WHITE ·· 1786 1ST EDITION OF HIS 'THE CABINET MAKERS & UPHOLSTERERS GUIDE PUBLISHED 1788, 2ND 1789, 3RD 1794	**W. & J. HALFPENNY Circa 1750** ARCHITECTS & DESIGNERS OF FURNITURE GOTHIC & CHINESE FATHER & SON WORKING TOGETHER
Thos SHERATON 1751·1806 1ST EDITION OF HIS 'THE CABINET MAKERS & UPHOLSTERERS DRAWING BOOK PUBLISHED 1791·1794	**Geo HEPPLEWHITE ·· 1786**
INCE & MAYHEW 1758·1810 1759–63 PUBLISHED 'UNIVERSAL SYSTEM OF HOUSEHOLD FURNITURE	**Wm HALLETT 1707·1781** MOST POPULAR CABINET MAKER DURING REIGN OF GEORGE II
HENRY HOLLAND 1746·1806 ARCHITECT· STRICT GRAECO·ROMAN STYLE .	**Wm & John LINNELL Circa 1720·1763**
Thos HOPE 1769·1831 PUBLISHED HOUSEHOLD FURNITURE & INTERIOR DECORATION 1807	**Geo SEDDON 1727· 1801**
Geo SMITH Circa 1780·1840 PUBLISHED 'A COLLECTION OF DESIGNS FOR HOUSEHOLD FURNITURE & AND INTERIOR DECORATION 1808	**Wm VILE & JOHN COBB** Circa 1750·1765 A MOST FAMOUS MANUFACTURING PARTNERSHIP
LE GAIGNEUR Circa 1815	**Wm INCE & JOHN MAYHEW** Circa 1758·1810
AUGUSTUS WELBY PUGIN 1812·1852 GOTHIC DECORATION ON HOUSES OF PARLIAMENT	**Robt & Thos GILLOW Circa 1740·1811** MAKERS OF FURNITURE ·LANCASTER & LATER (CIRCA 1760) LONDON
T. KING PRODUCED 'THE MODERN STYLE OF CABINET WORK 1839 LIKENED TO DESIGNS BY GEORGE SMITH AND THE LATER EGYPTIAN 'TASTE & CABINET WORK SUPPLEMENT	**MARSH & TATHAM 1795**
	LE GAIGNEUR Circa 1815 BUHL WORK **Geo BULLOCK Circa 1817** (BOULE)
H.W. & A. ARROWSMITH 'HOUSE DECORATOR & PAINTERS GUIDE ALL STYLES 1840	**T.B. JORDAN** WOODCARVING MACHINE 1845
HENRY WHITTAKER Circa 1847 DESIGNER	**MORRIS, MARSHALL & FAULKNER** & CO 1861
Chas EASTLAKE 1836·1906 HINTS ON HOUSEHOLD TASTE	**WARWICK SCHOOL OF CARVING** CIRCA 1850
BRUCE TALBERT DESIGNER·APPEARANCE OF MEDIAEVAL WOODWORK PEGGED JOINTS ETC	**GREAT EXHIBITION 1851** (STARTED)
RICHARD CHARLES DESIGNER	**HOLLAND & SONS** 23 MOUNT STREET · LONDON· EXHIBITED AT
E.W. GODWIN DESIGNER	**INTERNATIONAL EXHIBITIONS** PARIS 1855.1867 · LONDON 1862· 1871
CHRISTOPHER DRESSER JAPANESE TASTE	**J.G. GRACE & SONS 1745·1899** FAMILY FIRM

Time chart of principal designers and makers

INDEX

A number which is printed in italics refers to the page where an illustration appears.